MASTER YOUR FIRST JOB

THE REMARKABLE PATH FROM FIRST DAY TO FIRST PROMOTION

JACOB KARNES

ISBN: 979-8-89316-1-717 (paperback)
ISBN: 979-8-89316-1-700 (hardcover)
ISBN: 979-8-89316-1-724 (ebook)

DOWNLOAD THE AUDIOBOOK FOR FREE!

Thank you so much for buying my book. I would like to give you the audiobook for free!

I am a huge fan of audiobooks because they have significantly boosted my book completion rate. I narrated the audiobook myself so that the listening experience felt conversational.

Audiobooks normally cost between $10 - $25, but I would like to give it to you for free!

Download the audiobook for free here:
MasterYourFirstJob.com/Audio

GET A FREE VIDEO SUMMARY

I wish every book had a way for me to go back and get a high-level overview after I have read the book.

I created this video summary to do exactly that. In just 15 minutes, I cover the contents of this book at a high level so that you can remind yourself of the tools and master your first job.

In this video, I cover:

1. The tools you need to thrive in your first job.
2. How you can get your first raise and first promotion.
3. How you can use your first job to advance your career.

Get the video summary here:
MasterYourFirstJob.com/Video

DEDICATION

To my parents. I would not be where I am today without you both.
Thank you for making me get a job and apply to Chick-fil-A.

To my wife, Addi, and my daughter, Jamie. You are my
inspiration and joy. Thank you for believing in me.

CONTENTS

INTRODUCTION

A DECADE AT MY FIRST JOB

H ave you ever done something you didn't want to do? When I was 16 years old, I took a job that I didn't want. To be honest, I didn't feel like I was ready to even have a job. When you're young, you just want to spend as much time with your friends as possible. But I had a car, and if I wanted to put gas in it, I had to have money. My need for money became a need for a job.

I took a job with a company I didn't want to work for, in an industry I had no interest in. I was aware of the type of job I desired, and this wasn't it. I also had a clear vision for my life and career. So why was I accepting a position that didn't align with my future goals? What could I possibly learn from this job that would benefit me later in my career? Was this merely a waste of time?

If you're about to enter the workforce, or if you're already in your first job, you might resonate with my feelings. Perhaps you're in a role you didn't want or are questioning the value of your job. Like me, you might view it as a waste of time.

Conversely, if you're in the camp that enjoys your job and seeking success, you're likely exploring ways to excel and advance. You're curious about what it takes to move up the ladder and increase your earnings. You're trying to understand how your current role can be a stepping stone for your career.

I have experienced both perspectives at various times during my first job. I've been exactly where you are now—an employee feeling unfulfilled and apathetic.

After a decade, I can confidently state that I mastered my first job, and I'm eager to guide you in achieving the same success. That's why I wrote *Master Your First Job*. In this book, you'll discover how to become the employee everyone wants to hire, secure your first raise or promotion, and leverage your initial job for long-term success. You'll master ten key techniques that will not only benefit you in your current position but also support your career for years to come.

Starting my job at Chick-fil-A at 16, I never anticipated staying for ten years. Throughout that time, I acquired the life lessons and skills that I've shared in this book. I mastered my first job, transforming it into a springboard for career advancement. After a decade, I leveraged this foundation to start my own company, doing what I love, thanks to the insights and skills I've detailed in this book.

The lessons in *Master Your First Job* enabled me to earn my first raise, secure my first promotion, and unlock my first professional job opportunity, eventually leading me to establish my own business. I've achieved a healthy work-life balance and a fulfilling career, all rooted in the lessons from the initial ten years of my professional journey. I'm excited to share these insights with you to help you carve out a successful path in your career.

As you delve into this book, you'll discover how to become the exemplary employee that every employer seeks. The strategies and skills presented here are universal, applicable across all jobs, industries, and levels. You'll learn to seize the full potential of your initial employment, secure your first raise, and achieve your initial promotion. My goal is for you to emerge with a 'Master's Degree' in excelling at your first job.

I often reflect on how beneficial these insights would have been at the outset of my career. It took a decade to amass the wisdom and expertise necessary to excel in my first role. However, this book aims to expedite your learning process, equipping you with this knowledge now, sparing you years of trial and error. Embrace this opportunity to make the most of your first job—don't leave feeling unfulfilled or yearning for more.

By mastering your first job with the guidance offered here, you'll lay a solid foundation for your career, creating immediate and future opportunities for yourself. Turn the page, and let's embark on this transformative journey together!

CHAPTER 1

TAKE ADVANTAGE OF UNEXPECTED OPPORTUNITIES

"Go out on a limb. That's where the fruit is."
– President Jimmy Carter

THE JOB I DIDN'T WANT

I n 2012, when I obtained my driver's license, the excitement was palpable. This rite of passage, common for those turning 16, symbolized newfound freedom. The anticipation of driving, socializing with friends, and enjoying loud music was exhilarating. That Christmas, my parents presented me with a black 2001 Honda Accord in pristine condition. Remarkably, the car featured an audio system compatible with my phone—a rarity for a vehicle from 2001. The sense of joy and liberation was immense.

However, the car was more than a mere gift (with strings attached). Although it promised enjoyable times, its primary purpose was practical. At that time, as a high school junior, I was preparing for a senior year of dual enrollment, where I would attend a local university while still in high school, earning both high school and college credits. The car was essential for commuting between these two educational settings.

Owning the car also came with financial responsibilities. To cover the car payments to my parents, fuel, and insurance, I needed a job that accommodated my academic schedule and paid sufficiently. This job would enable me to manage these expenses and still enjoy the car's benefits.

I sought not just any job but one that I would find enjoyable. I pondered various questions about potential workplaces, including the type of jobs available to someone my age, the ease of the work, the pay, and the flexibility of hours. While considering options like fast food and babysitting, neither appealed to me—the former lacked excitement and the latter, consistency and familiarity among males. I also dismissed the idea of working at a car wash due to its unappealing nature and irregular hours. Then, a perfect opportunity struck me: working at a golf course.

Having played golf in high school from February to May, spending four afternoons weekly on the course, I was familiar with the environment and the staff roles. The tasks, including cleaning golf carts, assisting golfers, managing retail in the pro shop, and organizing equipment, seemed enjoyable. Additionally, the perk of playing free golf on my days off solidified my decision to pursue this opportunity.

I submitted applications to the three nearest golf courses, a process that involved obtaining, completing, and returning paper applications—a surprising method given the year was 2013. Expecting responses from at least two, I was puzzled when a week, then ten days passed without any communication. Considering my golfing experience, academic achievements, and strong work ethic, their lack of response was perplexing.

Meanwhile, my parents, concerned about the absence of car payments, urged me to apply to Chick-fil-A. Despite my reluctance due to its fast-food nature and its ubiquity as a first job in my hometown of Atlanta, I needed employment. After submitting a similar paper application at Chick-fil-A, they promptly contacted me for an interview, a stark contrast to the golf courses' silence.

The interview process at Chick-fil-A involved two stages, starting with a group interview where I and nine others answered various questions. Some inquiries were unconventional, highlighting the unique nature of their hiring process, such as:

> "If you were to describe yourself as one of Chick-fil-A's dipping sauces, which one would you pick and why?"

> "If you were to hire only one person other than yourself at this table, which person would you choose, and why?"

I successfully navigated the group interview at Chick-fil-A and progressed to a one-on-one interview, which felt more comfortable and focused on personal questions and my interest in the job. Upon being offered the position—a job I initially did not want—I faced a dilemma: accept the offer or hold out for a potential call from the golf courses.

Seeking guidance, I discussed my options with my parents, who, while eager for me to start working, provided thoughtful advice on the matter. Additionally, I consulted a friend who held a team leader position at Chick-fil-A, seeking insight into his experiences, which he described positively. To further clarify my thoughts, I listed the pros and cons of each option on paper.

After these discussions and careful consideration, I decided to accept the job at Chick-fil-A, despite feeling as though I was sacrificing my ideal job at a golf course. At the time, this felt like a significant compromise, but in retrospect, it proved to be a wise choice, illustrating the value of openness to unexpected opportunities.

HOW TO TAKE CALCULATED RISKS

Accepting the job at Chick-fil-A represented a significant compromise for me. Despite its lack of appeal, I recognized the necessity of the role for financial reasons, though it wasn't the enjoyable experience I had hoped for in a job. The emotional toll of this decision was palpable—I was grappling with the uncertainty of the choice's long-term impact.

In the realm of first jobs, confronting tough decisions is inevitable. These choices often involve risks, especially when the outcomes are unpredictable. Life's unpredictability means that a first job can present unforeseen opportunities. The key to navigating this uncertainty is engaging in calculated risk-taking.

Calculated risk-taking involves a thorough evaluation of potential outcomes. People's appetites for risk vary significantly—some are natural risk-takers, while others, like myself, are more risk-averse. However, when faced with career decisions shrouded in uncertainty, embracing some level of risk is essential. My aim is to guide you in transforming your approach to decision-making and risk-taking into a more deliberate and thoughtful process.

Here are three ways you can take calculated risks:

1. **Expect the Unexpected:** Life is full of uncertainties and inevitable difficult decisions. When your mind is open to encountering unexpected opportunities, you won't be thrown off-balance whenever one comes.

   Oscar Wilde said, "To expect the unexpected shows a thoroughly modern intellect."

   The first step in taking advantage of unexpected opportunities and taking a calculated risk is to expect the unexpected.

   When I think about taking advantage of an unexpected opportunity, I think about baseball players. Baseball players are never *truly* surprised whenever they get thrown a curveball. Why? Because they know the pitcher could throw one on any given pitch. The pitcher doesn't throw a curveball every time, and the batter never knows *exactly* when it's coming, but the batter knows that a curveball could come.

   You need to apply this same approach to life and work. Expect that an unexpected opportunity could come your way. If a batter never expected a curveball, they'd never get a hit. The best batters expect a curveball, and they hit it out of the park for a home run. So, if you want to be able to take advantage of unexpected opportunities, always expect the unexpected.

2. **Weigh the Possible Outcomes:** When I got the job offer at Chick-fil-A, I didn't know if the best thing to do was wait for the job I wanted at the golf course or to accept this one, even though I didn't want it. I decided to think about what could happen if I took that job at Chick-fil-A. So, I took a piece of paper, wrote "Positive Outcomes" and "Negative Outcomes" at

the top, drew a line down the middle of the page, and wrote out all the outcomes I could envisage.

When you have new opportunities in life or at work, it is crucial to think about what the positive and negative outcomes might be. Sometimes, the best thing to do is get a sheet of paper, draw a line down the middle, and write out the potential positive and negative outcomes.

When I did this, the answer to my decision became clear: I needed to take the job at Chick-fil-A. The potential positive outcomes I wrote down filled the page. The possible negative outcomes were only a few bullet points. Taking the job was a risk, but it was a risk worth taking because I had weighed the potential outcomes.

Weigh out your potential outcomes. Write it all down. You might be surprised by the result. If the possible positive outcomes outweigh the negative, this is an excellent opportunity to take a *calculated* risk. At least you'd know that your risk of failure is much lower than your chances of being successful.

3. **Ask Others for Wisdom:** I don't like asking for help, which might be my least favorite quality about myself. If you struggle with asking for help, I get it. Let me encourage you: please do it anyway! There are so many times in life and at work when you need help. The best resource is to ask someone who has been in your shoes before and who can give you wisdom.

   I first asked my parents. I trusted that they had my best interest at heart. They had been in my shoes seeking a first-time job before. I then went to my friend who worked at Chick-fil-A. I had known this friend for a long time, and he had worked at Chick-fil-A for a few years. My parents were older and wiser than me and had been in my shoes. My friend had also quite recently been in my exact situation, deciding whether to take a Chick-fil-A job or not. And my friend had two years of success after deciding to work there.

By seeking out others and asking for wisdom, you significantly improve your chances of taking advantage of unexpected opportunities and having a positive outcome. It's also one of the things you do to turn a risk into a calculated risk. If you are facing an unexpected situation and want to take advantage of it, seek wisdom. Do you know anyone who has been in your shoes before? Is there someone you trust who has your best interest at heart? Seek out these people and listen to their wisdom. They can help you make a wise decision.

Life is always going to throw you curveballs. You aren't going to get a hit every time, but I want you to be able to hit the curveball more consistently. When you seek advice from seasoned and experienced veterans, they will give you some tips and knowledge on how best to anticipate those unexpected curveballs. This way, your chances of hitting them increase. In the same vein, seeking advice from more experienced people helps you to properly calculate your risks before you take them.

Taking a calculated risk is the best way to take advantage of unexpected opportunities. By expecting the unexpected, weighing out the possible outcomes, and asking others for wisdom, you can become an expert at hitting the curveball.

THE JOB I NEEDED

After accepting my job at Chick-fil-A, I was nervous. I came in, filled out the annoying paperwork, and then collected my uniform. During my first few shifts, some of the leaders at the restaurant trained me, showing me what to do and how to do it. I even got to work with my friend during those first few weeks. As the days went by, one possible outcome crept into my mind: I imagined that I'd work at Chick-fil-A for a couple of weeks, and then the golf course would call me back and offer me a job. Would I just quit and go work for the golf course? Luckily for me, that didn't happen.

I worked at Chick-fil-A for a few weeks and enjoyed it. I loved the people, the culture, the attention to detail, the high standard of excellence, the speed of service, the hospitality, and the care that we showed guests— not customers—guests. I loved my job. It wasn't the job I wanted, but it was the job I needed.

What would "the job you need" look like for you? For me, Chick-fil-A checked a lot of boxes. I needed a job that could offer me flexible hours and decent pay so that I could pay for my car. Beyond that, I needed a job that allowed me to thrive. I wanted to believe in the company I was working for, and I needed an environment where I could grow. Chick-fil-A checked all those "need" boxes and several "wants" as well.

What do you need in a job? Think about this as you approach getting your first job. Does your job check your "need" boxes? I would write down three things you need and should look out for in a job. Differentiate between those needs and your wants. I wanted to work for a golf course because it was cool, but I needed an environment where I could grow.

As I worked my first job at Chick-fil-A, weeks turned into months and years. I worked there for a decade. It turned out to be not just my first job but my first career opportunity.

You may not work for the same company for ten years. The company you work for may not turn out to be a career place for you, but the principles and tools you'll learn in this book still apply. I got my first career opportunity because of my first job. It started because I took advantage of the unexpected opportunities that came with it.

YOUR NEXT STEPS

- ☐ **Open Up Your Mind:** Today, start teaching yourself to expect the unexpected. Get good at hitting the curveball.
- ☐ **Weigh Out All Outcomes:** If you are currently weighing a tough decision, start by weighing out all possible outcomes. This will give you insight into the right direction to take.
- ☐ **Seek Wisdom:** Reach out to someone who is older and wiser than you. Ask them for wisdom on whatever situation you are going through.

To master your first job, the first technique you need to practice is taking advantage of unexpected opportunities. To take advantage of unexpected opportunities, you have to take calculated risks. You can hit the curveball now that you're equipped with that mindset. The following technique is something every employer wants and needs from an employee, whether it's your first job or you're a 25-year vice president of a company: flexibility.

CHAPTER 2

FLEXIBILITY IS KEY

"Blessed are the flexible, for they will not allow
themselves to become bent out of shape."
– Robert Ludlum

THEY RUINED MY PLAN

Chick-fil-A hired me to work in the Front of House in the restaurant, the area you see when you first enter. This section was exciting to me because I felt I could perform best there, and it was where my friend worked.

In the Front of House, there are several roles. Cashiers or Front Counter Order Takers handle orders when you walk inside. Dining Room Hosts keep the dining area clean, refresh guests' beverages, and provide hospitality. Drive-thru Order Takers, or "headset" people, manage orders for the drive-thru, while the Window person takes payment and hands out orders. Baggers are responsible for packing the food neatly and ensuring the accuracy of orders. Lastly, there are Runners who serve dine-in guests.

I started as a Front Counter Order Taker and Dining Room Host, typical entry points for new team members. Interacting with guests and providing hospitality was exciting for me. I also challenged myself to see how quickly I could take orders and clean the dining area, as I'm highly competitive.

Within my first six months, I was trained in every position in the Front of House. I particularly enjoyed being a Bagger, as it's a role critical to the drive-thru's efficiency. Speed is essential, but so is accuracy, since it's crucial that guests receive the correct orders. Being an excellent communicator is also vital in this fast-paced environment.

However, a shift occurred when one of the managers mentioned that several team members in the Back of House had left. We needed more staff there, and he asked if I would consider moving. The Back of House is where all the food preparation happens, from prepping produce to breading chicken and cooking meals.

I was frustrated by this suggestion. I was growing to love my Front of House role and aiming for a promotion to team leader there. Moving to the Back of House felt like it would derail my plans and allow someone else to advance before me. Additionally, I perceived the Back of House as less prestigious and had fewer friends there, adding to my reluctance.

I felt I had no choice but to accept the transition to the Back of House, albeit with hesitancy. However, I communicated my concerns to my manager, expressing my apprehension about losing momentum and my ambition to advance within the company. My manager empathized with my situation, sharing his own experience of transitioning from the Front of House to the Back of House.

He explained that this move had allowed him to demonstrate his adaptability and positive attitude to the leadership team, earning their trust and respect, which eventually facilitated his own advancement within the restaurant. Encouraged by his story, I donned my new hat, slipped on some food-service gloves, and made my way to the kitchen.

HOW TO BE FLEXIBLE

You will need flexibility for the rest of your life, especially at work. Whether it's your first job or you're a 30-year career veteran, you need to be flexible. Flexibility is one of the most sought-after skills by every employer because everyone knows things will rarely go according to plan.

I first learned about flexibility and adaptability while growing up and playing sports. Sports are one of the best teachers because things can change instantly. In a football game, almost nothing goes perfectly according to plan. Each team is actively trying to disrupt the other team's plan, so the game is won by the team that best adapts to their plans being thwarted. When you miss a big chance, how will you respond? When you miss a block or drop a pass, can you move on to the next play? Teams with the most composure and ability to adapt almost always win.

Practicing flexibility in your first job will set you up for long-term success in your career. Flexibility starts with the mindset, and after you've ingrained it in your mind to be flexible, you have to start building habits around it.

When I think about flexibility and mindset, I can't help but think about Steven Covey's "Circle of Influence." In his book, *The 7 Habits of Highly Effective People*, Steven Covey discusses your "Circle of Influence" vs your "Circle of Concern." There are things outside your influence that may concern you, but you can't influence the outcome. On the other hand, there are things that concern you that you *can* influence.

In his chapter about proactivity, he goes one step further:

> *"The problems we face go in one of three areas: direct control (problems involving our own behavior); indirect control (problems involving other people's behavior); or no control (problems we can do nothing about, such as our past or situational realities)."*

Stephen Covey's book has inspired my approach to flexibility and how you can approach it at work to master your first job. I continue to apply it to my work by always asking three questions when a situation arises: What can I control? What can I influence? What can I neither control nor influence?

1. **What can I control?** You need to really think deeply about this—because there is almost always something you can control in any situation.

   One thing always in your control is your attitude and reaction. The problem is that situations that require us to be flexible usually evoke a quick reaction. So we must prepare ourselves and develop the habit of controlling our emotions, and reaction, because it only takes one lousy reaction for someone to lose trust in you.

   Whenever a situation comes up that requires flexibility, the first step is to pause, breathe, and remind yourself of the things you're in control of right now. Among everything, you are always in control of your attitude and reaction. Learn to keep a positive attitude and give a non-rebellious response.

   Sometimes, your employer or superior may make promises and fail to follow through. For example, your supervisor may suddenly start changing your job responsibilities despite promising not to change them when you got hired. What can you control? You can control your attitude, react positively, and remind them about what they promised you.

Sometimes, *the situation* may be out of your control, but control what you *can* control. Always pause and ask yourself, "What can I control?" You can almost always control *something*. Spend your time, energy, and emotions focusing on what you can control.

2. **What can I influence?** You asked yourself what you could control, and you answered and reacted accordingly. The next step is asking what you can influence. Is there something here that is beyond your complete control but still within your influence?

For example, maybe you're at work, and some co-workers are distracted and not paying attention to customers or their job responsibilities. You, on the other hand, are doing your job well, but now you have to work twice as hard to make up for the vacuum that their lack of effort has created. You can control what you are doing and still do your job. But you cannot control what they are doing. Can you influence it? Maybe.

If you're friends with one of them, you can influence the situation by talking to them. Ask them politely to put in more effort. At that point, you can't control how they react after you speak up, but there's a possibility that your words could influence them to become more attentive. Think about how much your boss would appreciate it if they find out that you were not only doing your job well, but you also influenced other employees to be more efficient.

Every employer is seeking an employee with high influence. And again, this doesn't only apply to your first job. Companies actively seek high-influence employees in high-paying careers at every level.

After asking yourself what you can control, control what you can control. After asking yourself what you can influence, influence what you can influence.

3. **What can I neither control nor influence?** This question is not the most challenging but the toughest one to respond to. If something is out of your control and out of your influence, then you have two options:

Pray it gets better.

Or

Let it go.

What typically happens is that when you encounter a negative situation at work that is beyond your control and influence, you may feel frustrated and react negatively. This underscores our initial point: it's crucial to manage your reactions.

If you find yourself unable to control or influence a situation, the best course of action is to let it go. This concept of 'letting go' is something I've grappled with throughout my life. To provide some context, I identify strongly with the Enneagram Type 8. For those unfamiliar with the Enneagram, a Type 8 is characterized as 'The Challenger,' 'The Protector,' or as I prefer to describe it, 'The Controller.' The core fear for Type 8s is a lack of control. Consequently, confronting situations where I lack control poses a significant challenge for me.

If you resonate with this struggle, particularly in situations where control is out of your reach, I understand completely. The truth is, such scenarios are inevitable in any career. One of the most valuable lessons I've learned—and continue to reinforce—is the importance of letting go in circumstances where I cannot exert control or influence. Focus on managing what you can—beginning with your emotions—and exert influence where possible.

Learning to let go of what you can neither control nor influence will inevitably lead to making some hard choices in your career. It might mean quitting your job or taking on a new role. You might also decide to roll with the punches and see where it takes you. When you do not have control or influence over a situation, you can pray it will get better. If it doesn't get better, then you have to let it go or move on to something different.

Always focus first on what you can control. Focus 75 percent of your effort in this area. Then, move on to what you can influence. Focus the remaining 25 percent of your effort in this area. Lastly, pray about and/or let go of what you can't control or influence. It's not worth your time. People don't remember how every situation affected each person. But they will remember how you react. Control what you can control. Influence what you can influence. And pray about what you can't control or influence.

FLEXIBILITY CAN BE REWARDING

I was initially hesitant to embrace my new role in the Back of House, yet I saw it as an opportunity to demonstrate my adaptability. Recognizing that my attitude was within my control, I maintained positivity despite my reservations.

Embracing my competitive nature, I challenged myself to become the epitome of hospitality and positivity in the Back of House. My goal was to stand out through exceptional kindness and an enthusiastic approach to teamwork.

I focused on influencing areas within my reach. Noticing a lack of emphasis on customer service in the kitchen compared to my experiences in the front, I aimed to inspire change. By consistently delivering top-quality food, I sought to elevate our standard of hospitality. At Chick-fil-A, where every customer's story is valued, ensuring excellent culinary experiences was my contribution to our guests' overall satisfaction.

Gradually, I observed a shift in my colleagues' attitudes and efforts, affirming that my dedication was indeed contagious.

While the decision to move me was beyond my control, this experience underscored the limits of my influence, particularly regarding my aspirations for advancement. The situation challenged my penchant for control, leading to a valuable lesson in focusing on what I could affect and releasing what I couldn't.

My biggest fear was remaining stuck in the Back of House, silently laboring in an unwanted role for months or even years. I dreaded the possibility of a deteriorating work ethic and attitude, fearing it might culminate in my resignation without ever achieving a promotion.

Fortunately, my experience unfolded differently. I spent six months in the Back of House, where, contrary to my initial apprehension, I found enjoyment. I thrived in various roles, particularly excelling in the "Sandwiches" station, where the complexity of assembling and packaging the menu item suited my strengths. This role allowed me to embrace the meticulous nature of the work, balancing speed with precision, and discover a newfound appreciation for this segment of the restaurant.

This period of flexibility demonstrated my team-oriented mindset to my supervisors, earning their respect and recognition. After six months, I transitioned back to the Front of House, feeling a mix of excitement and a hint of nostalgia for the back. My aim was to ascend within the Front of House, and soon after, my efforts were rewarded with a promotion to a leadership role.

My initial plan—to secure a promotion within my first year—did materialize, albeit through an unexpected route. The journey taught me the essence of adaptability and the power of controlling what's within my reach while letting go of what's not.

My second promotion was a direct result of my comprehensive experience, including my time in the Back of House, which proved invaluable. This unforeseen twist in my career path—what I once viewed as a derailment—ultimately paved the way for greater achievements.

The lesson here is this: as you navigate your career, embracing flexibility ensures resilience. You'll remain adaptable, never thrown off course by the unpredictable nature of job roles.

YOUR NEXT STEPS

Take out your notebook, phone, or wherever you take notes, and answer these reflection questions. Or write your answers right here in the book.

☐ **Reflection Question:** What's one thing in your control that you could work on to help you be more flexible?

☐ **Reflection Question:** What's one thing in your circle of influence that you could affect to help you be more flexible?

☐ **Reflection Question:** What's one thing not in your control or influence that you need to pray about or let go of to be more flexible?

You can take advantage of unexpected opportunities by becoming a calculated-risk-taker. By learning what's in and out of your control, you can master flexibility. The following tool you can use to help you master your first job is a little spark that you can use to ignite your passions: curiosity.

CHAPTER 3

DARE TO BE CURIOUS

"We keep moving forward, opening new doors, and doing new things because we're curious, and curiosity keeps leading us down new paths."
– Walt Disney

RUNNING OUT OF OPPORTUNITIES

The more I immersed myself in my role at Chick-fil-A, the more I enjoyed it. I was proactive in seizing the opportunities presented to me, embracing the shifts in my responsibilities with agility. Yet, the deeper I delved, the more I aspired to achieve. My appetite for knowledge and experience seemed insatiable.

This drive is fundamental to my nature. I'm inherently motivated and fully committed to areas where I excel or have a strong interest. However, professional growth at a job can sometimes encounter barriers. At Chick-fil-A, I reached such a barrier. Despite my eagerness to advance and expand my skills, I found the limits of what my role could offer in terms of growth. My performance was consistently high, yet I was becoming disengaged.

With no promotional paths open and having explored lateral moves within the restaurant, my frustration and boredom escalated, edging toward apathy—a topic we will explore in the upcoming chapter. I was determined to maintain my enthusiasm and pursuit of developmental opportunities. Thus, I initiated conversations.

I inquired with colleagues and leaders, asking, "What can you tell me about your role?"

Occasionally, I stayed beyond my shift or spent breaks engaging with others to understand their responsibilities. My curiousity opened new avenues of knowledge.

Leadership roles intrigued me, particularly the critical task of ordering and managing inventory, a role pivotal to our service delivery. However, that position was not within my reach.

I also explored the recruitment aspect, recalling the group interview conducted by one of our managers when I was hired. While the idea of conducting interviews piqued my interest, offering a chance to utilize my discernment, no opportunities were available in that area.

Training was another area that captured my interest, particularly the idea of developing onboarding systems to enhance new employees' initial experiences, potentially improving their retention and job satisfaction. Yet, this too was beyond my current scope.

Eventually, a discussion with a manager broadened my perspective to consider the entire Chick-fil-A organization, not just our individual location. We discussed the brand's growth and national expansion. This conversation sparked a pivotal question:

> "Are there opportunities for me at Chick-fil-A beyond this restaurant's four walls?"

The answer was yes.

CURIOSITY OPENS NEW DOORS

From my early years, curiosity has been a defining trait of mine. My mother can recount numerous instances of my relentless questioning during childhood, many of which have turned into amusing stories we cherish today. Despite the cautionary saying "curiosity killed the cat," my experience has been quite the opposite; curiosity has consistently opened new avenues for me. It's akin to a persistent itch that only intensifies the more you scratch.

We are all endowed with unique skills, abilities, interests, and passions that shape our individuality and influence how we allocate our time. These traits ignite our curiosity, a natural inclination to explore further when we encounter areas that resonate with our interests or strengths. In the workplace, when topics align with our passions or talents, our curiosity is inevitably piqued, urging us to delve deeper, much like attending to an irresistible itch.

This profound sense of fascination and zeal is beneficial. It doesn't lead to any proverbial fatalities among felines. Echoing Walt Disney's words from the start of this chapter, curiosity acts as a key, unlocking new opportunities and guiding us along uncharted paths. However, it's common in professional settings to encounter voices or circumstances that discourage this explorative spirit. It's crucial to disregard such deterrents, as succumbing to them could foster apathy.

Embracing your curiosity can significantly enhance the value and personal growth derived from your initial employment experiences. It serves as a gateway to your preferences, passions, and essence, transforming work into a more enjoyable and fulfilling endeavor. By engaging in tasks that align with your curiosity, you're likely to become a more committed and content employee. Therefore, the question arises: How will you embrace curiosity to excel in and derive the most satisfaction from your first job?

1. **Ask Questions:** I've heard, "There's no such thing as a bad question!" But that's not true. You *can* ask the wrong question. The first step in asking questions is figuring out *what* to ask. The next step is figuring out *who* to ask. The last step is figuring out *when* to ask.

   My brother-in-law worked his first job at a golf course, managing the course and landscape. He got really curious about the science behind getting the grass to be in prime playing conditions for golf. His curiosity was so high that he decided to start asking questions. He had to ask the right questions to the right person at the right time.

   My brother-in-law knew that the right person to ask was his boss. His boss had a degree in turf management and knew all the science behind keeping the course in good shape. He figured the best time to ask was when he wasn't in the middle of an important task. His boss typically had some downtime toward the end of his shift. Then was the hard part—getting the courage to ask the right question.

   He caught his boss at the perfect time and asked, "Can I shadow you and come watch how you keep this course in such great shape?"

My brother-in-law did all three things very well. He asked the right person the question, found a perfect time, and asked an excellent question.

He didn't just walk up to his boss and ask, "How do you keep the course in such great shape?"

That would have been counter-intuitive. He had more to the question that he was asking. He wanted to learn how to do it and to observe. He didn't just want to hear a verbal answer. So, he asked the right question to the right person at the right time.

Asking this and other clear questions has led him to change his degree and career path because he was curious. By asking good questions, we can turn curiosity into an open door.

2. **Show Initiative:** If curiosity is a feeling, initiative is an action. Showing initiative is a great way to show your employer that you are serious and willing to act on something you are curious about. While I would love for you to work for the best boss who can see you are curious from a mile away and offer you opportunities without you having to ask, the reality of that happening is slim.

   To transform curiosity into a gateway for opportunities at work, taking initiative is required. Reflecting on my brother-in-law's experience, his proactive approach is a prime example of initiative in action. By requesting to shadow his boss for deeper learning, he demonstrated a strong initiative characterized by two key elements: desire and effort.

   Initiative begins with expressing your desire. When you actively voice your willingness to undertake additional tasks, it signals your eagerness to engage more deeply. This expression of interest is likely to encourage your boss to nurture and challenge that enthusiasm. Engaging in tasks that excite you not only results in higher quality work but also leaves a positive impression on your superiors.

Effort is the next critical component of initiative. Demonstrating your work ethic is about taking concrete steps and showing dedication. Success in your career is not handed to you; it must be earned through diligence and proactive behavior. This principle is vital in your first job. Ambition alone is insufficient; it must be coupled with action. My brother-in-law exemplified this by arriving early and dedicating himself to learn and grow in areas that piqued his curiosity. Such actions illustrate a robust work ethic and a commitment to personal growth.

By showcasing both desire and effort, you signal to your boss that you're not just interested but also prepared to invest in your development. This blend of initiative can effectively convert your curiosity into new possibilities at work.

3. **Try Something New:** You won't know until you give it a shot. There's a bit of mystery and excitement in stepping through a new door, curious about what's on the other side. Trying new things is a bit like an adventure—you might not always end up liking what you find, but that's no reason to stop exploring.

    As an adult, I've become quite the enthusiast for sampling new foods. There's a whole world of flavors out there, some that might not initially appeal to you but could end up being delightful. And then there are those that promise a feast for the senses but fall short on taste. It's all part of the adventure. My foray into different cuisines has enriched my palate and introduced me to some incredible tastes I would have missed had I not been willing to experiment.

Think of trying new things as grabbing unexpected opportunities. You've already got a taste of this idea from a previous chapter.

While not every new experience will be a hit, each one is a step forward in discovering what you enjoy and what you don't. It's all about the journey and the surprises you find along the way.

I've encountered numerous individuals who've taken new career directions, spurred by a simple yet powerful force: curiosity. Their stories share a common thread—they all began with a flicker of curiosity, a moment when something caught their eye and piqued their interest. What distinguishes those who find success from those who harbor regret is the subsequent step: taking action.

Those who look back with regret are the ones who paused at curiosity. They experienced that initial spark but chose to suppress it, remaining stagnant. They saw a glimpse of a path unfolding but didn't pursue it.

Conversely, those who transformed their curiosity into opportunity are the ones who actively sought more information. They didn't just wonder; they acted. They asked pertinent questions of the right people at the opportune moment. Demonstrating initiative, they made their interest and dedication evident. By embracing new experiences and diving into uncharted territories, they opened doors to new possibilities and paths.

AN OPEN DOOR

I was intrigued by potential opportunities at my Chick-fil-A. I took considerable initiative, arrived early, and stayed late, driven by a desire to learn. Despite my diligence and substantial effort, I didn't find new opportunities. Nevertheless, when I began posing the right questions to the right people at opportune moments, things started to change.

This led to a revelation about the Certified Trainer program. I would spend a week at Chick-fil-A's headquarters, The Support Center, learning to train others for the company. This role would enable me to travel nationwide, training new team members at grand opening Chick-fil-A restaurants.

Eager, I inquired about participating. The most negative outcome would be a rejection, which seemed a minor risk. Fortunately, I was allowed to join the program, which ushered in numerous opportunities. My initial visit to The Support Center was extraordinary, revealing the extensive team effort behind our restaurant's success.

The Marketing department crafted strategies across various levels, while Field Operations, which included the role of Operations Lead, maintained a vital connection with the restaurants. The Talent team managed recruitment, hiring, and onboarding at The Support Center. Simultaneously, Learning and Development devised essential training resources, including the digital platform Pathway, for restaurant team members like me.

I encountered numerous individuals at The Support Center, discovering their roles. Among them were professionals in a building called "The Nest," where they designed Chick-fil-A's then-new table markers. These markers addressed a common challenge for team members like myself: efficiently locating guests to deliver their orders. During a visit to The Nest, I expressed my aspiration:

"I would love to work in this building one day."

Fast forward four years, I secured a position at The Support Center, operating daily in The Nest.

One of the best things that happened while being at the Support Center was meeting a participant in the Leadership Development Program

(LDP). He managed training and grand openings at new Chick-fil-A locations across the country. He became a confidant, later supervising my training assignments. Our collaboration on eleven grand openings in seven states cemented our bond. Over time, he evolved into a close friend and mentor, guiding me from my initial role to a fulfilling career.

On a personal note, this friend introduced me to the woman who would become my wife. She was a colleague in his prior position at a Chick-fil-A restaurant. Our mutual connection led to me meeting my wife. At the time of this writing, my wife and I have celebrated five years of marriage and have a two-year-old daughter.

Participation in the Certified Trainer program invigorated my role at my restaurant. Post-training, I returned re-energized, applying insights from grand openings to enhance our service's speed, precision, and warmth. My inquisitiveness didn't just enrich me; it also elevated our team's performance.

Curiosity isn't detrimental; it unlocks opportunities. My eagerness to grow propelled me to seek answers, take initiative, and embrace new experiences. This curiosity spurred nationwide travels, enhanced my workplace, forged lasting friendships, introduced me to my spouse, and transformed a job into a career.

Embrace curiosity. Venture to unlock new possibilities.

YOUR NEXT STEPS

If you are curious about something at work, I encourage you to do these three things:

- ☐ **Show Initiative:** Schedule a meeting with the right person at work to ask them questions about the topic you're curious about.
- ☐ **Ask Good Questions:** Ask the right person the right questions at the right time. Write these questions down ahead of time so that you don't shoot from the hip when you have the meeting.
- ☐ **Try Something New:** If your conversation isn't productive, that's okay. Try something new. If your discussion is fruitful and opens a new door, walk through it and try something new.

You've now learned three techniques. To master your first job, take advantage of unexpected opportunities, practice flexibility, and dare to be curious. It eventually happens to everyone, so you've got to ask, "What happens when I hit the wall at work?" In the next chapter, let's talk about how to handle apathy.

CHAPTER 4

FIGHT APATHY

"The greatest danger to our future is apathy."
- Jane Goodall

GETTING BORED

aim to spotlight a pivotal chapter from my tenure at Chick-fil-A: the interim between exhausting growth avenues and discovering the Certified Trainer program, as discussed previously. I omitted it initially to dedicate an entire chapter here due to its significance. Amidst the lull, the scarcity of growth opportunities, and ultimately identifying a solution, I encountered apathy.

As mentioned before, my drive to improve and advance at work was strong. I was on the lookout for chances to enhance my performance, assume additional responsibilities, secure promotions, and increase my earnings. Roughly eighteen months in, I confronted apathy for the first time.

I had excelled in my role, yet I sensed no further progression available. My aspiration was to advance and evolve, but no promotions were available for me. How could I stay motivated to grow without the prospect of promotion? Once more, I felt hindered.

Earning more was a goal. While I could request a raise, I hesitated, unsure how to articulate my worth to my supervisor. I lacked clear reasons for deserving more pay beyond my competence in my role. Lacking the prospect of getting a raise, apathy persisted.

Days turned repetitive, filled with identical tasks. I believed I merited opportunities for growth and improvement but found none. Boredom ensued, and beyond that, a diminishing care. Each morning's awakening brought no excitement for work. I experienced what Patrick Lencioni terms "Sunday Blues"—not resentment toward my job, just disinterest.

Externally, my demeanor didn't reveal my inner turmoil. I maintained a smile, interacted warmly with colleagues and guests, and performed competently. Despite working diligently, I wasn't meeting my own standards. No one inquired about my well-being or recognized my internal struggle.

Mentally, I was in a dismal place. Being inherently driven, I questioned this unexpected emotional void at work. My ambition was to continue progressing and achieving my objectives.

I was entitled to opportunities for advancement and self-improvement. I deserved a way out of apathy, to be motivated, and to harbor positive sentiments about my work. Yet, I lacked a strategy, a path forward, and guidance on whom to approach for assistance.

HOW TO FIGHT APATHY

Apathy signifies an absence of emotion, not aligning with positive or negative feelings but embodying a state devoid of any emotional engagement. This condition is perilous, as reaching a point of indifference to outcomes—whether good or bad—is detrimental to one's mental health. Apathy can foster a deep-seated dislike for your job, hinder your professional development, and curb your ability to realize your full potential.

Engaging in monotonous, unvaried tasks daily can inevitably lead to apathy. Your progress may stagnate, growth can decelerate, and dissatisfaction will likely ensue. The ensuing boredom and motivational deficit are precursors to apathy. Therefore, it's crucial to acknowledge the potential onset of apathy and devise strategies to combat it proactively. How can you brace yourself for apathy's eventuality and muster the resilience to counteract it when it arises?

1. **Ask for Help:** Seeking assistance is profoundly underappreciated and should be embraced more frequently. Many perceive requesting help as a sign of weakness, yet it can be a formidable asset during challenging times. By seeking support, you demonstrate vulnerability, an act of courage that underscores strength, not frailty.

   Combating apathy begins with reaching out for help. Whom can you approach? Identify a trustworthy individual, someone genuinely concerned for your well-being and invested in your best interests. This person might be the advisor you turned to in chapter one. If you have someone in your life who embodies these qualities, cherish and maintain that connection.

   Such a confidant is invaluable, particularly when you confront workplace apathy. Approach this trusted individual for support.

Articulating your feelings may be challenging, but express your emotions as clearly as possible. Whether it's a lack of feeling, frustration, or sadness at work, share your experiences. Discuss your aspirations and delve into the root causes of your apathy.

The strength found in community and the act of sharing your struggles is immense. Confiding in someone equipped to assist can be a vital strategy in your arsenal. By asking for help, you can prevent apathy from escalating into a more severe issue.

2. **Cultivate Work Relationships:** You technically don't have to be friends with anyone you work with. You're all there to do a job, and you're all getting paid. As long as the job is getting done, I guess you don't *have* to be friends with anyone there. But I can tell you from experience that work is a lot better when you get to do the job with your friends.

    I've always heard the phrase, "Misery loves company." That's true, and that's true when apathy sets in. It can be healthy to go through that with someone else, and you can share your experiences. The opposite is also true. Joy loves company as well. Having fun at work is much more fun when you do it with someone else.

    Comradeship plays an essential role in the workplace. Experiencing shared situations with colleagues can act as a preventative measure against apathy. Enjoyable interactions with friends at work can make minor annoyances seem less significant. Moreover, when apathy does arise, having friends to discuss and navigate through these feelings with can be incredibly beneficial.

    Make an effort to establish friendships at work. Often, our lifelong friendships form simply because we share common spaces and experiences with others. For many, the closest friendships have originated from school or church interactions. Similarly, the workplace provides a fertile environment for cultivating meaningful relationships. The bonds you form at work can serve as a vital antidote to combat workplace apathy.

3. **Find a Project:** Finding a project to work on within your job might be quite difficult, but it's a surefire way to fight apathy. A book that has had an impact on my life is Viktor Frankl's *Man's Search for Meaning*. In his book, Frankl argues that humanity's ultimate motivator and desire is to find meaning.

Viktor Frankl's expertise in finding life's meaning is deeply rooted in his harrowing experiences. As a Jewish Austrian who endured three years in Nazi concentration camps, losing nearly all his family to the Holocaust, Frankl's insights into human resilience and the quest for meaning are profound. Despite the immense personal losses, he maintained a belief in the intrinsic meaning of life, which forms the cornerstone of his therapeutic approach, Logotherapy.

In the context of your work, applying Frankl's principles can be a powerful antidote to apathy. Logotherapy suggests that engaging in a meaningful project can provide a sense of purpose and fulfillment. When you're tasked with a specific objective, meeting milestones, and facing deadlines, it propels you into action, countering feelings of indifference or lack of motivation.

To combat workplace apathy, consider initiating a project, no matter the scale. For instance, if you're employed at a car wash and notice customers struggling with the floor mat cleaning machine, devising a clearer instructional sign could be a simple yet impactful project. This approach not only addresses a practical issue but also instills a sense of accomplishment and purpose.

By finding a project at work, you create a "mini job" within your role, leading to a feeling of fulfillment upon its completion. This sense of achievement and purpose are vital tools in your arsenal against apathy. Therefore, whenever you feel disengaged or unmotivated at work, seek out a project to rekindle your sense of purpose and combat apathy effectively.

As highlighted at this section's outset, apathy poses a significant risk, necessitating effective strategies to counteract it. Engaging in help-seeking behavior, particularly when feeling apathetic or even depressed, is challenging yet crucial. Embracing vulnerability, contrary to being perceived as a weakness, is indeed a formidable strength. Seeking assistance provides access to insights and strategies essential for combating apathy.

Nurturing relationships in the workplace is vital. Initially, you may perceive your role as merely needing colleagues, not close friends. However, fostering connections and establishing a supportive community at work can be instrumental in mitigating apathy. Shared experiences often breed empathy, enhancing the workplace environment and providing a network of support.

Embarking on a stimulating project is another effective antidote to apathy. The inherent human drive to be productive means that engaging in meaningful tasks can alleviate feelings of boredom or disengagement. Identifying a project or task that resonates with you can instill a sense of accomplishment. This sense of achievement is a powerful remedy for apathy, replacing it with fulfillment and a renewed sense of purpose.

CLIMBING OUT OF THE HOLE

I didn't want to let apathy ruin my time at work, so I searched for ways to overcome it. By this point, I had become friends with my colleagues. Did they feel the same way I did? After spending a few months concealing my apathy, I confided in some of my closest work friends to see if they ever felt similarly. Some were in the same situation, while others had not experienced it yet. However, we were all facing the same work environment, so being surrounded by people who understood my situation and were in a better place benefited me.

Subsequently, I sought wisdom and shared my feelings about work with my parents. They had my best interests at heart and could offer sound advice. They listened empathetically, understanding my mental state. They made me feel seen and heard, sharing their own experiences of feeling the same way in their jobs. But they didn't stop there; they offered help.

They reminded me that I was most motivated in school when I was engaged in sports. That resonated with me. I knew I was always more motivated and happier when busy with something I enjoyed. I needed to be too busy to feel apathetic. I needed a project. Finding a project was challenging because I felt I had reached the limits of my role.

However, I refused to let apathy win. I began to investigate. Were there initiatives at other Chick-fil-A locations that we hadn't tried? Could I introduce a new system? I needed to find something that would help me overcome apathy. Fortunately, I discovered a new trend at Chick-fil-A: a system called "outside order taking" or "iPOS" that was being introduced nationwide.

If you've visited a Chick-fil-A, you've likely seen this. Team members take your order face-to-face in the drive-thru. When I was there, this was a novel concept. Yet, the statistics on the productivity gains from outside order taking, when implemented effectively, were impressive. This new drive-thru system could enhance order accuracy, speed of service, and guest hospitality—a triple win.

After researching, I prepared and pitched the idea to my bosses. They approved it, recognizing its potential benefits and cost-effectiveness for our business.

Implementing the face-to-face outside order-taking system in our drive-thru became one of my favorite projects at Chick-fil-A. I collaborated with vendors, garnered support from team members, ordered equipment, and established new systems.

Once operational, our drive-thru became one of the top-performing in the state, using internal metrics to gauge its effectiveness. The system's success inspired other restaurants, including Zaxby's, In-N-Out Burger, Raising Cane's, and McDonald's, to adopt similar methods. I took pride in initiating and implementing this system at my restaurant.

The deeper I dove into the project, the less apathetic I felt. My search for a project began because I sought help. Engaging more with my coworkers and sharing experiences diminished my apathy. I was too occupied with the project and building relationships to feel apathetic. Apathy is a real issue, but by seeking help, finding a project, and fostering workplace relationships, you can combat apathy effectively.

YOUR NEXT STEPS

If you are struggling with apathy at work, don't just sit around and wait for it to phase out. Fight it by taking these steps starting right now:

- ☐ **Tell Someone How You Feel:** The first step in fighting apathy is admitting you feel it to yourself and to someone who can help you. Ask them for help. Asking for help is one of the bravest things you can do.
- ☐ **Cultivate Your Work Relationships:** Going through a shared experience with someone can be highly bonding. Allow yourself to cultivate your work relationships so that you never feel alone at work.
- ☐ **Find a Project to Work On:** The project can be big or small. Do some research or ask your boss if there's a project you can do to take something off their plate. Whenever you accomplish a project, you become more fulfilled. Whenever you feel fulfillment, you'll feel the apathy recede.

You have now learned four techniques that will help you excel in your first job: seizing unexpected opportunities, practicing flexibility, embracing curiosity, and combating apathy. When tackling apathy, remember to seek help, leverage your work relationships, and engage in meaningful projects. Now, it's time to elevate your approach. How can you make a lasting impression and be remembered for your unique contributions at work? Turn the page to discover how!

CHAPTER 5

BUILD YOUR BRAND

"When you really understand who you are,
it enables you to fight and believe."
- Phil Knight

WHAT AM I KNOWN FOR?

I became a team leader about a year and a half into my tenure at Chick-fil-A. My responsibilities included managing shifts, coordinating breaks, and ensuring my area was clean at the end of each day. Another colleague and I were promoted at the same time, and we often ran shifts together. We had developed a strong friendship and shared similar approaches to managing our respective areas of the business.

Upon becoming a leader, I aimed to stand out. I wanted to imprint my personal touch on shifts and make a noticeable difference when I was in charge. I observed that the team's morale, speed, efficiency, and hospitality varied depending on the shift leader.

I aspired for my shifts to be distinctive. Driven by a healthy sense of pride, I was determined to provide guests with exceptional service when I was present. I pondered over what my unique stamp on shifts would entail. Holding myself to a high standard of excellence, I valued efficiency and strived for the best, wanting my shifts to be a reflection of these qualities.

One of the most significant challenges for any new leader is earning the trust and respect of their team. There are colleagues who might feel they were more deserving of the promotion. Some may harbor resentment from before your promotion, while others might prefer the previous leaders and their methods.

I was aware of the challenges ahead, as I sought not only to be trusted, respected, and liked but also to enforce my way of doing things and instill my standard of excellence.

My leadership journey began under challenging circumstances. Two other leaders had abruptly resigned on a Saturday, and I stepped into the leadership role the following Monday. These leaders had set lower standards than I aspired to; they were content with "good enough" and met only the minimum requirements. They did not prioritize speed or accuracy and favored leaving early over maintaining cleanliness.

I was determined not to continue in this vein. I aimed to make a significant impact on my shifts and uphold high standards, regardless of others' indifference.

However, this led to considerable resistance from other team members, as higher standards meant more effort was required from them. This was a new expectation, and it positioned me unfavorably in their eyes. I faced a dilemma between upholding my standards and being liked by my colleagues. Rallying the team to embrace higher standards was an arduous task, and at times, the burden seemed to fall on just a few of us, making me question the worth of my efforts. The temptation to abandon my pursuit of distinctiveness was strong, leaving me to wonder about the point of it all.

BUILDING A BRAND

I am a big fan of branding. I am fascinated by how companies create an atmosphere and reputation that becomes like their second identity. When top-level professionals create a brand, you can look at the simplest version of a logo and know exactly who they are and what they're about. These brands even evoke emotion whenever you think about them. When I find a brand I love, I become incredibly loyal to it. There are a few examples of brands that I love that do this well: Nike, Disney, and Apple.

Phil Knight, the founder of Nike, created a brand in a market dominated by larger brands, but Nike stood out. They gear their advertisements toward inspiring you to become something more extraordinary. Nike now collaborates with some of the best athletes and is the largest shoe brand in the world. Nike's logo is the Nike Swoosh. When you see the Swoosh, you know exactly what it is and what brand it represents.

The Swoosh itself isn't unique. Phil Knight paid a Portland State graphic design student $35 for the logo in 1971. It's just a modified checkmark-looking thing. It used to have the word "Nike" above the Swoosh on all branding, but Nike has become so well-known that you don't need to see the letters N-I-K-E to recognize the Swoosh. The logo isn't special in itself, but Nike has created a memorable brand, and the Swoosh represents that brand.

We can say the same about Disney. When Walt Disney created his signature decades ago, it wasn't particularly memorable. But the Disney brand would later become remarkable. His signature "D" and his little mouse would become internationally recognized symbols of an iconic brand. Whenever you see the Disney "D" or a circle with two smaller circles at 10 and 2 o'clock forming the shape of Mickey Mouse's head, you instinctively associate it with the Disney brand.

How about Apple? Apple entered a computer space dominated by Microsoft and IBM. It was the small fish in a big pond but has created an iconic brand with iconic products. Even beyond their recognizable logo, there are design elements so purposefully woven throughout Apple's products that when you see a phone, computer, headphones, or a watch that looks a certain way, you know it's from Apple. The legendary designer Sir Jony Ive intentionally crafted brand elements that are distinctly Apple.

What about your brand? What does your brand look like? What do people think of when they see your name? I knew what mine looked like and how I wanted to represent myself. Does this matter at your first job? To master your first job and advance in your career, you must know and represent your brand well. How can you build your brand?

1. **Discover Your Brand:** The first step in building a personal brand is to discover your brand. The process of self-discovery can be easy for some and hard for others. How can you discover your personal brand? Look deep within you. Your God-given talents, abilities, and interests are what make up who you are. We just have to get them out on paper.

    One great way to do this is through personality tests. You can choose from a ton: The Enneagram, DISC, CliftonStrengths, Working Genius, Myers-Briggs, 16 Personalities, etc. You really can't go wrong with any of them. There are free and cheap options for all of these. Take one or several of these tests. Look at the results. Does this describe who you are or who you want to be? If so, start writing down every word or phrase you like that comes from these results. If you disagree with the results, take a different test and find one you do like.

Not everyone is fond of personality tests. Some feel they are restrictive, boxing individuals into predefined categories. However, I believe personality tests are valuable tools for self-discovery. They provide language to articulate who you are and help clarify who you aspire to become.

I encourage you to jot down every word or phrase from the test results that resonates with you. Store them on your computer, phone, a sheet of paper, a whiteboard, etc. Don't worry about having too many words at this stage. We'll refine this list later. For now, save all the words that speak to you.

Consider using an AI tool to expand your vocabulary. For instance, as an Enneagram Type 8, I could ask the AI,

"Give me 25 adjectives that describe an Enneagram Type 8."

Now, I have 25 additional words to consider. Apply this method with various personality tests you undertake. Leverage modern tools to enhance your understanding of your personal brand.

Take your time with this process. Personality tests can be enlightening, offering deep insights into your character. Allow yourself to engage fully in this journey of self-discovery and begin crafting the best version of yourself.

2. **Refine Your Brand:** Now that you've compiled your list of words or phrases from personality tests, it's time to refine your brand. When I undertook this exercise, I began with over 50 words or phrases that I felt represented my brand. The next step is to refine and prioritize.

Prioritization is crucial because if everything is deemed most important, then effectively, nothing is. Some attributes must stand out more than others. Our ultimate goal is to distill your list down to three key words or phrases. Start by eliminating or crossing out the less critical words and phrases, and consider merging similar ones. This process should help you reduce your list to approximately ten items.

Once you have your top ten words or phrases, the challenging part is to further narrow this down to just three that encapsulate your brand. Merge where possible and deeply consider what is truly essential. After selecting your three, arrange them in order of importance. Not all can hold equal weight—one should emerge as the most pivotal.

For instance, in my role as a Business Coach, I define my brand with these three ranked phrases:

1.   Coach's Mindset
2.   High Standard of Excellence
3.   Ruthlessly Efficient

This trio encapsulates how I wish to present myself in my professional endeavors. I aim for clients to recognize my coach's mindset and my commitment to their success, to observe the high standards I uphold, and to experience my efficiency in action.

Now, what does this look like for you? Dedicate time to refine your brand down to three key phrases and rank them by significance.

By distilling your brand to these three core elements and ranking them, you equip yourself with a concise and impactful way to articulate your personal brand when asked.

3. **Represent Your Brand:** Now that you've established your brand, the long-term goal is to embody it consistently. However, in the short term, you need to set yourself up for success. Start by sharing your brand with a coworker or friend. Explain how you intend to represent yourself. This not only adds a layer of accountability but might also encourage them to undertake a similar journey. Remember, having an accountability partner typically leads to greater success.

   Next, discuss your brand with one of your leaders. Explain your choice and its significance to you. This conversation will achieve two things: firstly, it demonstrates your enthusiasm and initiative to your boss; secondly, it introduces another level of accountability. You might even motivate your leader to consider their personal brand if they haven't already.

   Finally, the responsibility to live out your brand lies with you. Keeping your brand visible, perhaps written down where you can see it daily, acts as a constant reminder of who you aspire to be. When you've shared your brand aspirations with others, they can help keep you on track. Ultimately, the most crucial factor is your commitment to actively and consistently represent your brand.

Branding is a fascinating concept. Some companies have mastered their branding to the extent that their logos alone stir emotions. Whenever I glimpse the Disney mouse ears or the "D" logo, I'm transported back to childhood, reliving trips to Walt Disney World. I reminisce about taking my daughter there, watching her marvel at Main Street. Such profound emotions, all triggered by a simple logo, underscore the power of branding.

Similarly, your personal brand can evoke distinct feelings in others. When colleagues see your name on the work schedule, what will their immediate reaction be? Will they be thrilled to work with you, or will they regret not taking the day off? By identifying, honing, and embodying your brand, you have the power to influence these perceptions.

LEAVING A MARK

I reflected on who I was and who I aspired to be. After taking some personality tests, including Myers-Briggs and DISC, I discovered I was an INTJ on Myers-Briggs and a DC on DISC. I identified some of my strengths and jotted down words that described me. This process of self-discovery was incredibly beneficial, helping me understand myself better and envision the best version of myself.

While at Chick-fil-A, I deliberated extensively about my desired brand. I sifted through various words and phrases, refining my brand. I identified myself as fast, clean, efficient, ultra-competitive, and having high standards. Consequently, I had a list of about 20 words that seemed crucial. My aim was to represent myself positively while also creating an enjoyable environment for others. Ultimately, I distilled my brand down to three core aspects: a high standard of excellence, efficiency in task completion, and caring for others. This became my mantra for how I would conduct myself and manage my shifts.

The initial weeks were challenging. Our team worked later than usual as we began cleaning more thoroughly. We faced growing pains while implementing new, efficient systems that demanded more effort from our team. During this period of instilling my personal brand into the shifts, I wasn't the most popular leader.

Despite initial resistance, the team gradually began to appreciate the new approach. This shift wasn't coincidental; while I upheld a high standard of excellence and expected diligent work, demonstrating care was vital. I made a concerted effort to integrate "care" into my brand, ensuring my team felt valued.

During my shifts, I focused on running a smooth operation while also dedicating time to understand my coworkers better and learn about their lives. By showing genuine concern and explaining the rationale behind the changes, we fostered a sense of camaraderie. The team became more engaged and enjoyed their work.

The other leader and I earned positive reputations for our shift management. Our service was quicker, our hospitality scores improved, and the restaurant was cleaner under our supervision. Despite the increased workload, our team was content and engaged. We had fun and performed well, setting our group apart with a distinct brand.

Our primary concern with implementing changes was the potential for unpopularity. However, I didn't want to compromise my authenticity for approval. By incorporating "caring for people" into my brand, I provided the support my teammates needed to align with the brand, making it easier to make a lasting impact. Work became enjoyable, and I felt fulfilled by effectively establishing and living out my brand.

When people saw my name on the schedule, they had a clear expectation of the upcoming shift, whether they viewed it positively (as most did) or negatively (as a few did). They knew what to anticipate because I had successfully cultivated a personal brand. I took pride in my brand and have continued to leverage this approach throughout my career.

YOUR NEXT STEPS

- ☐ **Take Personality Tests:** There are plenty of free and cheap options. Write down all the words and phrases about your "type" you like and want your brand to be. You'll learn a lot about yourself and others in the process.
- ☐ **Narrow Down Your Three:** When you have your list of 25 to 50 words or phrases, I want you to narrow down your brand to your top three things. Rank them in order. This step is important because you can't represent 50 things well consistently. But you can represent three things well consistently.
- ☐ **Tell Others and Represent Your Brand:** Share your personal brand with a co-worker and a leader at work. Both parties can help hold you accountable for representing your brand well. You'll gain some respect from your leader. Lastly, it's now on you to represent your brand well.

You are halfway done learning the necessary techniques to master your first job. You've learned to take advantage of unexpected opportunities, be flexible, be curious, how to fight apathy, and now, you've built a personal brand.

Take some time to celebrate. Share what you've learned with others, and write down some reflections from this book so far. The following few chapters are hyper-focused on growth and contain tools that you will use to master your first job and advance your career years from now.

CHAPTER 6

STAY COACHABLE

*"My best skill was that I was coachable. I was
a sponge and aggressive to learn."*
- Michael Jordan.

A STEP-DOWN

About four and a half years into my Chick-fil-A journey, I moved from metro Atlanta to Gainesville, Florida, for two main reasons. First, I started dating my now-wife, who lived in Tampa, Florida. When a job opportunity in Gainesville arose, I was thrilled to reduce the distance from nearly seven hours to just under two hours away from my girlfriend. This move significantly benefited both my time and my gas budget. Secondly, this job represented a promotion for me.

Eager to build a career at Chick-fil-A, I sought experience at the highest leadership level. At the Gainesville location, my new boss offered me a directorial position. This role placed me at the pinnacle of leadership within the restaurant, reporting directly to the Owner/Operator. As one of three key leaders, I was a "number two" in the business hierarchy. Moreover, it was the grand opening of a new restaurant, allowing us the freedom to establish everything according to our preferences.

I committed to this role for six months to assist in launching the restaurant and ensuring its successful setup. We believed that this timeframe would suffice to stabilize the location and train other leaders to manage the business effectively. After six months, I faced a decision to either extend my stay or depart. Initially, I anticipated my time in Gainesville wouldn't exceed a year, as my relationship with my girlfriend was progressing seriously. My goal was to relocate to Tampa, become engaged, and marry.

During my tenure in Gainesville as the Director of Hospitality, I oversaw all Front of House operations. This responsibility entailed managing leaders, team members, performance metrics, restaurant cleanliness, systems, and scheduling for the Front of House. It was a challenging role, demanding yet rewarding.

While I had previously led other leaders, this directorial role required me to fully own a business segment, an experience that brought significant pressure and necessity for growth. I gained invaluable insights from my boss, who had successfully navigated a similar path to owning her business. The initial six months unfolded differently than anticipated, compelling me to adapt my business management approach.

My half-year in Gainesville was challenging, yet profoundly developmental. I am deeply grateful for that period, which was filled with memorable commutes to Tampa, advanced leadership lessons, and critical learning experiences from my boss on what it entails to be an Owner/Operator. I honed my skills as a director, learning to steer the business toward high-level achievements and lead both people and results effectively at Chick-fil-A.

After fulfilling my six-month commitment, I relocated to Tampa to be closer to my girlfriend, prioritizing our relationship above all else. Eager to continue my career at Chick-fil-A, I applied for several positions in Tampa, aiming for a directorial role that I believed I had earned through hard work and dedication. However, I encountered a significant challenge: despite my qualifications and experience, I was only offered entry-level Team Member positions, which would result in a demotion in both leadership status and salary.

Persistence paid off when I found a Chick-fil-A willing to offer a compromise, though it still involved a pay reduction and a lower-level leadership role. This position came with the promise of growth and advancement opportunities, prompting a difficult decision about balancing my career aspirations with my personal life priorities.

Ultimately, I accepted a position in the Tampa–St. Petersburg area and moved to Tampa. Joining a new team as the "new guy" was daunting, especially since I was already familiar with Chick-fil-A's operations. The experience felt somewhat demeaning, as I was stepping into a role I had already mastered, surrounded by colleagues who might have less experience.

Before starting, I met with my new boss, who advised me to approach the job with humility, integrate well with the team, and remain open to coaching. He was acquainted with my previous supervisor and aware of my capabilities, offering reassurance and support as I transitioned into this new role.

Despite this encouragement, adapting to the new job was challenging. While I intended to embrace humility, I struggled internally with being perceived as less experienced and receiving well-meaning but unnecessary advice from colleagues unaware of my background. I frequently noticed areas for improvement, reinforcing the feeling that I had more to contribute than my new position allowed.

As far as I know, I never acted arrogantly on the outside. It was just in my thoughts. I worked hard to remain humble. I worked hard to get to know my new co-workers. And I tried—*I really tried*—to stay coachable.

THE GREATS ARE COACHABLE

Many regard Michael Jordan as the greatest basketball player of all time—the GOAT. While I, a LeBron fan, believe the definition of "greatest" can vary, there's no denying Jordan's status as one of the premier athletes in any sport. This chapter opens with a quote from Jordan, who attributed his coachability as his most significant asset.

Jordan's basketball skills were extraordinary, from his exceptional ball handling and passing to his smooth mid-range jump shot and unparalleled vertical ability for his size. Beyond his physical skills, his mindset set him apart: a competitive drive like no other, using any possible means as motivation, cementing his legacy as a legendary winner and the so-called GOAT. Yet, when reflecting on his talents, Jordan highlights not these attributes but his receptiveness to coaching.

What lesson can we draw from this? If a figure as illustrious as Michael Jordan values being coachable, then it's a trait we should all aspire to cultivate. Being coachable means being amenable to learning and improving, particularly within your professional sphere. Embracing this quality not only enhances your current performance but also arms you with a lifelong skill that will benefit your entire career. So, what are the steps to remain coachable in your workplace?

1. **Practice Humility**: While Michael Jordan is renowned for his basketball prowess, he's equally famous for his trash-talking

on the court, often targeting specific opponents throughout games. This behavior doesn't necessarily reflect humility toward his adversaries. However, Jordan did exhibit humility in his interactions with coaches, distinguishing his attitude in competition from his approach to learning and guidance.

Humility is a valued virtue in the workplace, so much so that employers can discern its absence or presence, potentially as early as the interview stage. Therefore, cultivating humility is not just beneficial but essential for your career progression. True humility starts with a mindset shift—without genuinely humble thoughts, humble actions are difficult to manifest.

To me, humility involves showing care and consideration for others, adopting an "I am second" attitude. This perspective is echoed in the teachings of Jesus in the New Testament, who, despite his divine status, emphasized and practiced humility. His instructions to "turn the other cheek" and "if someone asks you to go one mile, go with them two" encapsulate this virtue.

In my studies on humility, Jesus's example stands out, demonstrating how to live and work with a genuine sense of humility. By prioritizing the needs and desires of others, you not only make humility more accessible but also more noticeable to those around you. Recognized humility in your interactions can garner respect from peers and superiors alike. Importantly, humility is a foundational element of coachability.

2. **"Listen as if You Are Wrong"**: Recently, a leader advised me to "Talk as if you are right, but listen as if you are wrong." This guidance seemed straightforward at first, yet its depth unfolded with further contemplation. It significantly influenced my approach to conflicts, meetings, and discussions on various topics or ideas.

The initial part—talking as if you're right—came naturally to me; I felt confident in my views most of the time. If I harbored doubts, I likely wouldn't voice my opinion. For those who find it challenging to express disagreement or share ideas, I urge you to speak up. Your insights and contributions are valuable, particularly in a professional setting. If you struggle with this, start practicing. Speaking confidently can lead to acknowledgment and can catalyze positive changes when issues are raised or ideas are shared.

However, for individuals like me, who can debate fervently on any subject, the real challenge lies in the second part of the advice: listen as if you might be wrong. It's one thing to articulate your views assertively, but it's another to genuinely consider others' perspectives with the openness to being incorrect. This was particularly challenging for me. Do you find it difficult as well? Try genuinely listening, open to the possibility that you might not have all the answers.

I discovered that during discussions, I often focused more on formulating my next argument rather than truly listening. When I made a conscious effort to listen more intently, I encountered an enlightening realization: sometimes, I was wrong. Listening with the humility to acknowledge potential errors opens the door to new perspectives and fosters a growth mindset—a belief that your abilities and understanding can develop with effort and open-mindedness. But what exactly is a growth mindset?

3. **Have a Growth Mindset:** Growth mindset is a term that comes from Dr. Carol Dweck. She is a leading mind when it comes to growth mindset. In her book, *Mindset,* Dweck defines growth mindset this way:

"This growth mindset is based on the belief that your basic qualities are things that you can cultivate through your efforts, your strategies, and help from others. Although people may differ in every which way—in their initial talents, aptitudes, interests, or temperaments—everyone can change and grow through application and experience."

When you have a growth mindset, you believe you can get better. Contrary to a growth mindset, there is a fixed mindset. Dweck defines a fixed mindset as the opposite:

"believing your qualities are carved in stone." The juxtaposition between the two couldn't be more significant.

When you harbor a fixed mindset, believing that your abilities are static, it inevitably influences how you respond to coaching. This mindset leads to resistance against feedback, often being perceived as arrogance. In such a state, when you receive feedback, it's likely to be dismissed, as you're convinced that no improvement is possible.

Conversely, adopting a growth mindset transforms your approach to coaching. Embracing the belief that you can develop and enhance your skills makes you more receptive to coaching. With a growth mindset, you view coaching positively, as an opportunity for growth, and you're seen as humble. Feedback, under this mindset, is not just criticism but a valuable resource, a gift that aids your development. (I'll delve deeper into this aspect shortly.)

Cultivating a growth mindset is crucial not only for becoming more coachable but also for achieving success in your job and broader career. Implementing this mindset fosters career advancement, enhances your receptivity to coaching, and establishes you as a collaborative team member whom others are eager to work with.

Even the most outstanding athletes exemplify coachability. The realm of sports is a frequent reference point in discussions about coachability, largely because it's an environment where the coach-athlete dynamic is pronounced. Observing top athletes in any sport can provide valuable insights into how they engage with their coaches. The most exceptional athletes display humility, listen intently, often with the assumption that they have something to learn, and adopt a growth mindset, acknowledging that there is always room for improvement.

When it comes to receiving coaching in your professional environment, aspire to emulate these athletes. Approach advice or feedback with humility, recognizing the value in others' perspectives. When engaged in discussions, confidently express your views while remaining open to the possibility that you might be incorrect. Embrace a growth mindset, understanding that your abilities and skills are malleable and capable of enhancement.

MOVING UP

Embracing coachability was a significant challenge for me. The initial step, maintaining a humble attitude, went smoothly. I treated my new coworkers with kindness, fostering good relationships. However, the second step, listening as if I might be wrong, proved more difficult. My team offered advice on tasks I had performed countless times, unaware of my extensive experience with Chick-fil-A, longer than many of them.

Resisting the urge to dismiss their suggestions, I chose to listen and learn, discovering that their methods—though different—were superior in efficiency and accuracy. This realization underscored the value of remaining open to new ideas, even in familiar territories.

The ultimate hurdle was adopting a growth mindset in a role I perceived as fully mastered. Despite my experience, acknowledging that there was still room for improvement was pivotal. By genuinely believing in the potential for growth and actively pursuing it, I enhanced my proficiency and demonstrated increased coachability.

This transformation facilitated a rapid promotion to a director role, a decision that, while potentially contentious among longer-tenured staff, was justified by my adaptability, teamwork, and potential. This advancement was crucial in propelling my career toward a corporate ambition with Chick-fil-A, a goal achieved within 15 months, largely attributable to my demonstrated coachability.

Echoing Michael Jordan's sentiment, coachability is an invaluable asset. It's imperative to cultivate this skill early in your career and maintain it throughout, as it fosters trust and respect from employers and peers alike. By staying humble, listening earnestly, and embracing a mindset of continuous improvement, you position yourself for success and recognition in any professional endeavor.

YOUR NEXT STEPS

- ☐ **Be Humble:** Arrogance won't fly at any job, and if you want to master this job to set you up for success in your career, start practicing humility now.
- ☐ **Listen as if You Are *Wrong*:** At work, if someone offers you advice or a different way to do things that go against what you think is right, listen as if you are wrong. Talk to them as if you're right, but listening as if you are wrong is essential.
- ☐ **Have a Growth Mindset:** This starts internally. Believe that you can grow and be better. This doesn't minimize your skills and talents—it actually maximizes them.

You've now learned about taking advantage of unexpected opportunities, being flexible and curious, fighting apathy at work, building your personal brand, and being coachable. Using these techniques at work will accelerate your career. Our next step is to take coachability to the next level. To be coachable, you have to accept feedback as a gift.

CHAPTER 7

FEEDBACK IS A GIFT

"If we shield ourselves from all
feedback, we stop growing."
- Brene Brown

RECEIVING TOUGH FEEDBACK

I began my journey at Chick-fil-A in 2013, initially viewing it as a mere job for extra income. However, my affection for the company led me to stay for a decade. My ambition extended beyond serving indefinitely as a team member or leader at a restaurant; I aspired to forge a lasting career with Chick-fil-A. My options were twofold: become an Owner/Operator and own my own Chick-fil-A franchise or pursue a role at the corporate headquarters, known as The Support Center.

Initially, the idea of being an Owner/Operator appealed to me. The prospect of running my own enterprise, especially in partnership with a brand like Chick-fil-A, was enticing. A pivotal moment came when a mentor posed a thought-provoking question: "Would you rather devise a system that addresses a problem for one restaurant or create a solution benefiting 3000 restaurants?" This question steered my career trajectory toward The Support Center, motivated by the desire to impact a broader scope of businesses.

My goal evolved into securing a position at Chick-fil-A's corporate office. The company's interview process is notably extensive and rigorous. After a comprehensive evaluation to determine my compatibility with the organization, my ambition was realized in 2019 when I was offered a role at The Support Center. Transitioning from nearly seven years at a restaurant to a corporate position, I gained invaluable insights into communication, professional presence, and leadership.

At Chick-fil-A, I participated in the Training Development Program (TDP), designed to equip emerging leaders from restaurant operations with the skills necessary for corporate success. This program was instrumental in my transition, providing a deep dive into the corporate realm and accelerating my career advancement.

In TDP, I undertook the role of a corporate trainer, a step up from my previous training experiences at restaurant openings. This role involved educating new franchise Owner/Operators and staff across various corporate levels. The stakes were high in TDP, given the significance of our audience and training content. Consequently, we adhered to rigorous feedback systems to ensure our training met the highest standards of excellence.

I considered myself proficient in both giving and receiving feedback, particularly excelling at the former. As someone who identifies with the Enneagram 8 personality type, I was known for not shying away from difficult conversations. In my previous role, I was the go-to person for delivering tough feedback and handling challenging customers, maintaining detachment in emotionally charged situations.

However, my entry into the Training Development Program (TDP) challenged this self-perception. The program quickly revealed gaps in my abilities to give and receive feedback. As I embarked on my new role, the initial confidence I had began to wane. The TDP onboarding and training—a two-week intensive—focused on honing our training skills, adapting content for various audiences, and striving for excellence in delivery. This process included observing seasoned TDP participants, emulating their delivery, and then receiving critique aimed at achieving top-tier results.

My first training attempt during onboarding was a pivotal moment. After replicating a session delivered by a tenured participant and adding my personal touch, I felt reasonably satisfied with my performance, despite finishing two minutes ahead of the intended ten-minute duration. The subsequent feedback session was structured to start with self-assessment, followed by peer and leader evaluations, focusing first on strengths and then on areas for improvement. While I acknowledged my timing issue, I believed there wasn't much else to critique.

The feedback I received, however, was extensive and focused significantly on areas I needed to improve—lasting nearly as long as the session itself. This experience was particularly jarring, as I had considered myself receptive to feedback. The intensity and volume of the criticism were unexpected and profoundly affected me, worsening my self-critical nature and diminishing my self-esteem.

This experience in TDP not only highlighted my discomfort in receiving feedback but also prompted a realization about my approach to giving it. I was more inclined to focus on the negatives, neglecting to recognize and highlight the positive aspects of someone's performance. This imbalance led me to a critical insight: I had fundamentally misunderstood the nature of feedback, perceiving it as predominantly negative rather than as an opportunity for balanced improvement. This realization forced me to confront and reassess my approach to feedback, acknowledging the need for a more constructive and balanced perspective.

Two weeks into my new role, I confronted a humbling realization: my skills in giving and receiving feedback were not as proficient as I had believed. Fortunately, as part of my onboarding process, I participated in a session aptly named "Feedback is a Gift." This session was transformative, teaching me to perceive feedback not as criticism but as a valuable gift meant for growth and improvement. Embracing this perspective significantly enhanced my ability to both offer and accept feedback effectively. I only wish I had come to understand and appreciate this concept earlier in my career, as it profoundly changed my approach and mindset toward feedback.

GIVING AND RECEIVING FEEDBACK

There are many feedback models available, and I'll delve into the one I learned. But before exploring this particular model, its benefits, and how it can enhance your job experience, let's discuss the significance of feedback.

Feedback is a crucial tool for growth and advancement. Whether it's internal or external, feedback is fundamental to development and progress. What exactly is feedback? Often, the term evokes negative connotations, but feedback isn't inherently negative or bad. It's essentially information provided in response to an action or behavior. This information can range from highly positive to critically negative, or fall anywhere in between. Thus, as we examine feedback, remember it can be positive, negative, or neutral. It's simply data on how things are perceived or performed.

This is precisely why feedback is vital. We require information to progress, whether it concerns you, an idea, a project, or a team. We need insights on how things are progressing. Take my cooking, for example. I cook frequently for my family and rely on their feedback to improve. If a dish doesn't taste good, I want to know so I won't repeat the mistake. Conversely, if a meal is a hit, that's valuable to know as well, encouraging me to stick to the recipe. Without positive feedback, I might unnecessarily alter a successful recipe trying to enhance it.

Now that we understand what feedback is and its importance, let's focus on how to provide effective feedback. Your team can greatly benefit from more individuals like you offering constructive feedback. By delivering valuable and thoughtful feedback, you gain the trust and respect of your peers and leaders, and they'll be grateful for your contributions. So, how can you offer beneficial feedback at work?

1. **Identify the What:** When you are giving feedback, my number one rule is that you have to be specific. The first step in giving good feedback is identifying what you want to emphasize. Again, this can be positive, negative, or anything in between. The most important aspect of identifying the "what" is that you are specific.

   If you are giving someone feedback, and you say something like:

   "You did an excellent job today."

   How is this information helpful? You are giving them information, sure. However, the information is vague and lacks context. How can the person you are providing feedback to move forward with this information?

   Let's go back to my example about cooking for my family. If my wife told me:

   "This meal could be better."

How is that helpful? It isn't really. I know the meal needs to improve, but I have no idea what was wrong with it. A better piece of feedback would be

"This meal is too salty."

This is an excellent example of identifying the "what." It's specific information about the meal, and I now have the context to use it moving forward.

Let's go back to telling someone they did a great job today. Stop and ask yourself, "What did they do well today?" Maybe you work at a golf course, and one of your co-workers was hospitable to the golfers and made some people's day. How would you give them feedback and identify the "what?"

You might say, "I noticed how kind you were to the golfers today. People were smiling after you talked to them. Great job!"

Do you see the difference between that sentence and the one above? The first one didn't identify the "what." The feedback was vague. The second feedback was specific and clearly identified the "what." To give good feedback, you must first identify the "what."

2. **Explain the Why:** After you have clearly identified the specific information you want to share, you want to give context. Why does the information you are sharing matter? What's the point? Without this, no one will take action from the information you give them.

You gave someone information, and it was specific. Why does it matter? By explaining the why, you add context and clarity to the information you share. You help people understand the exact thing they did right or wrong or could do better. Providing this clarity is an act of kindness and helps people to grow and get better.

Let's use an example with a piece of negative feedback. Let's say you work in retail at a boutique. Your co-worker is in charge of cleaning their area at the end of the shift, picking up trash, folding clothes, and cleaning the floors. You notice your co-worker does a quick fix when it comes to the floors instead of cleaning them the right way. First, we identify the "what."

"Hey, I noticed you swept the floors but didn't mop them."

That was specific and identified the "what." Now, we need to explain the "why." Why does this matter?

"When the boss comes in, and notices that the floors aren't cleaned properly, he will make me mop it."

Do you see how the "why" in this example is clear? Your co-worker not doing their part will affect you directly, so it's essential to clearly identify the what and explain the why. You are specific with information and explain why the feedback is so important.

3. **Create an Action Plan:** When giving feedback, it's crucial to identify the specific aspect of the person's work you're addressing and clarify its importance. Subsequently, you must provide a plan. What steps should they take now that they have this feedback? This guidance is vital because, without it, individuals may be uncertain about which behaviors to continue or discontinue.

What are the expectations moving forward? Addressing this question is essential during the feedback process. By outlining a future plan, you help paint a vision of a better future that the recipient is motivated to achieve. Omitting this step leaves recipients unsure about how to act on the feedback they've received.

Consider a positive scenario: Imagine you're a barista and have a colleague renowned for their efficiency in making beverages. Start by identifying the behavior and explaining its significance.

"Your efficiency in preparing beverages is impressive. Despite the fast pace, you never compromise on quality, which simplifies everyone's workload and prevents the need for remaking drinks due to consistent quality. Excellent work!"

This feedback highlights specific positive behaviors and explains their importance. The next step is to provide a plan for the future, which, in this case, is straightforward:

"Please continue your efficient work; your efforts are highly valued!"

Providing an action plan makes positive feedback actionable. Applying this to negative feedback is theoretically straightforward but can be more challenging in practice. Revisiting the earlier example of floor cleaning, an action plan for this feedback might look like this:

"Please ensure you thoroughly clean the floors before leaving and avoid taking shortcuts in the future."

By specifying the next steps, feedback becomes much clearer and more actionable. Effective feedback integrates three key components: identifying the behavior, explaining its significance, and outlining a plan for the future.

Giving feedback is a task that's easier said than done, necessitating courage, confidence, and emotional intelligence. To foster a productive mindset for providing feedback, it's beneficial to consider feedback as a gift. When you perceive feedback as a gift, you're more likely to deliver it effectively.

Consider how you handle a gift. You wouldn't toss it at someone; instead, you'd wrap it thoughtfully. Gifts are given with consideration and care, often to those we value. Feedback should be delivered in a similar manner—carefully packaged, delivered with consideration, and stemming from a genuine concern for the recipient.

Shifting focus to receiving feedback, how can one view feedback as a gift? It begins with mindset adjustment. Rather than interpreting feedback, particularly negative feedback, as a personal attack, recall the principles from the previous chapter: stay coachable. Listen with the openness to change and the acknowledgment that there may be areas of improvement.

To effectively receive feedback as a gift, it's helpful to receive well-constructed feedback. However, not everyone may utilize an effective feedback model like the one you've been taught. So, how can you ensure that the feedback you receive is constructive?

You can apply the feedback model I've described by asking insightful questions. If the feedback provided is vague, seek specifics by asking them to define the "what." What exactly are they addressing? Request clarification to ensure you fully understand their points.

Next, inquire about the significance of their feedback. Ask "why" questions to delve into the reasoning behind their feedback, ensuring you comprehend its importance.

Finally, seek guidance on future actions. Request an actionable plan: what changes are needed, or what behaviors should continue? Clarify these expectations with the provider.

By actively engaging in the feedback process, using the model you've learned for giving feedback, you can also enhance the quality of feedback you receive. When you receive well-structured feedback, you're better positioned to embrace it as a gift, fostering personal and professional growth.

ACCEPTING FEEDBACK AS A GIFT

As I continued my journey with TDP at the Chick-fil-A Support Center, I honed my skills in giving and receiving feedback. I learned to view feedback as a valuable gift. My greatest challenge was internal; I was acutely aware when my work fell short of expectations, and I was harsh on myself. Receiving criticism after a poor performance was the last thing I wanted.

During my time in TDP, I underwent extensive training. I trained in a program called Licensee, where we trained hundreds of restaurant leaders across the country via virtual sessions. We broadcasted our training live from the test kitchen at The Support Center, mimicking the authentic restaurant atmosphere prevalent in Chick-fil-A restaurants nationwide. Our setup included a complete film set, production crew, cameras, screens, lights, and microphones—it was an impressive arrangement.

The first time I led a session in this program, I was unsuccessful. It was my least effective training session in TDP, a fact I was painfully aware of.

When it was time to receive feedback, I had to live by the principles I advocated and accept the criticism graciously. The feedback was harsh: my presentation was mechanical, I attempted to imitate someone else's style, which only diminished my confidence in the material and my presence on camera. Additionally, my timing was off.

The rationale behind this feedback was clear. Given the challenges of virtual learning, it was imperative to make our sessions enjoyable, inject our personalities, engage dynamically, and maintain precise timing to ensure the audience benefited. Moving forward, I formulated an action plan focused on infusing more of my authentic self into the sessions, boosting my confidence, and making the experience more enjoyable and engaging for the participants.

Instead of wallowing in self-pity, I devoted myself to improving my session. I stopped trying to emulate others and instead brought my unique style to the forefront. The subsequent session I led turned out to be one of the most enjoyable and successful ones I've ever conducted.

I was no longer mechanical; I was confident. My personality shone through on camera, the timing was impeccable, and I genuinely enjoyed myself. This positive change resonated with the audience, making the session more enjoyable and effective for them as well. Consequently, the Licensee program transitioned from being my least favorite to my preferred training program.

I even developed a "catchphrase" that became my signature while training. I would discuss the "Jimmy's and Joe's" and the "Xs and Os," drawing an analogy between the need for skilled athletes and a solid playbook in sports to having the right talent and effective systems in a restaurant setting. To reinforce this point, I would don a "coach's hat" and sport various Georgia Football visors, emulating Coach Kirby Smart on the sidelines.

By embracing feedback as a valuable gift, I was able to transform my approach and succeed as a trainer.

Learning to give and receive feedback as a gift is transformative. It empowers you and others to excel and rectify counterproductive behaviors. It can transform your workplace into a more enjoyable and productive environment. Effective feedback involves identifying the issue, understanding its significance, and developing a forward-moving plan. When delivered thoughtfully and constructively, feedback truly becomes a gift.

YOUR NEXT STEPS

- ☐ **Practice Giving Good Feedback:** Identify the "what," explain the "why," and create a plan moving forward. Wrap the feedback up as a gift and handle it with care.
- ☐ **Ask for Feedback:** Ask a leader or someone you trust for feedback on your work performance.
- ☐ **Accept Your Next Feedback Conversation as a Gift:** If you aren't clear on the feedback, ask clarifying questions to understand the "what," "why," and what you need to do moving forward.

You have now learned seven techniques: taking advantage of unexpected opportunities, being more flexible and curious, combating apathy, building a personal brand, staying coachable, and giving and receiving good feedback.

While you are well on your way to mastering your first job, the tools you've acquired are just as vital now as they will be 25 years into your career. Next, let's delve into a topic that everyone finds exciting: how to increase your income.

CHAPTER 8

HOW TO GET A RAISE

*"Be a yardstick of quality. Some people aren't used
to an environment where excellence is expected."*
– Steve Jobs

I DESERVE A RAISE

You've now reached a topic that likely excites you: how to increase your income. To boost your earnings, the first step I recommend is mastering the seven tools we've already discussed. Applying these tools will make you an exemplary employee, invaluable to your employer.

Asking for a raise can be daunting. I recall a time early in my Chick-fil-A career when I felt deserving of a raise but was uncertain about the steps to secure it. After a year with the company, I believed I was a significant asset, yet I struggled with how to demonstrate my worth and the approach to request a raise. These questions, possibly familiar to you, were swirling in my mind.

Interestingly, most of my colleagues seemed indifferent about pursuing a raise, which left me questioning whether it was contentment or similar internal battles that deterred them. This lack of action made me feel somewhat guilty for believing I deserved more.

Why did I feel entitled to a raise? I observed my contributions and saw a distinct difference: my presence on a shift meant a quicker team, more accurate orders, and a cleaner restaurant. Despite being a novice leader, I was delivering superior results compared to my peers, directly benefiting the business's profitability. This led me to conclude that my value justified a higher compensation.

However, I was at a crossroads, unsure of the next steps or whom to seek guidance from. Discussions about salary seemed taboo in the workplace, an unspoken rule, leaving me in a predicament. Despite the general reluctance to talk about earnings, isn't financial motivation a common driver? My desire to earn more was clear, but the path to achieving it was not.

HOW TO ASK FOR A RAISE

Many employees desire higher earnings but don't actively pursue opportunities to increase their income. While it's common to want more money, simply working hard isn't enough; you need to take initiative and create opportunities to distinguish yourself within your organization.

It's important to acknowledge that while many feel deserving of higher pay, not everyone's actions warrant a raise. Job roles often have salary caps; for example, as a team member at Chick-fil-A, expecting a six-figure salary isn't realistic. However, surpassing your current earnings is feasible.

The 'secret sauce' to earning more is straightforward: contribute economic value to your organization. This principle is rooted in a basic business concept: a company's ability to pay its employees is linked to its profits. More revenue means more funds for salaries, while less income tightens budget constraints.

Employers aim to maximize profits, so if a business doesn't increase its earnings but raises salaries, its profit margins will shrink, jeopardizing its sustainability. Therefore, to secure a raise, you must demonstrate how you've boosted the company's revenue and profits.

The challenge lies in quantifying your contribution to the organization's economic value. I've developed a strategy to help you articulate your impact and effectively request a raise. While I can't promise specific outcomes since I'm not your employer, following these guidelines will significantly improve your chances of earning more.

1. **Meet with Your Boss**: The initial step in advancing your career and potentially increasing your income is to set up a meeting with your supervisor. If you report to multiple bosses, choose the one who has the most influence over compensation decisions or can provide critical insights you need.

    When arranging this meeting, it's common for your boss to inquire about the meeting's purpose. Rather than directly stating it's about a potential raise—which might lead to preconceived notions—it's more strategic to express your desire to discuss your professional growth and opportunities within the organization.

This approach is not deceptive; it aligns with your ultimate goal. The meeting is indeed about growth and development, which are foundational steps toward justifying a future raise request. This session is about gaining clarity and forming a strategy for your career advancement, not immediately asking for a raise.

By proactively seeking this discussion, you demonstrate your commitment to the company and your desire to contribute more significantly. The key is to frame the meeting as an opportunity to explore how you can evolve and excel within the company.

2. **Clarify Value:** As you prepare for this important meeting with your supervisor, it's essential to meticulously plan your approach. I recommend jotting down the questions you intend to ask in a notebook. Despite being a proponent of digital tools myself, using pen and paper during the meeting conveys professionalism and attentiveness more effectively than typing or scrolling through your phone. By arriving prepared, with questions written down and a readiness to take notes, you'll demonstrate your commitment to your role and the significance you place on this opportunity for dialogue.

What questions should you formulate? Our objective is to explore avenues for your growth and advancement. Begin by inquiring about your current performance. Embrace the concept from the previous chapter: view feedback as a valuable gift. In this context, constructive feedback can be instrumental in enhancing your earning potential.

Next, focus on understanding how you can contribute additional economic value to the company. Elevating your economic impact is a pivotal strategy for increasing your income. Furthermore, consider inquiring about ways to enhance cultural value within the organization. Although more challenging to measure, a positive corporate culture can significantly influence profitability.

By addressing these areas, you'll gain insights into how you can evolve professionally, increase your value to the company, and ultimately position yourself for financial growth.

Here are some example questions you can ask for each category:

Feedback
These questions are designed to delve deeply into your performance and areas for growth. As you engage in this discussion, remember the lessons from the previous chapter: focus on identifying specific aspects of your performance ('what'), seek explanations to understand the significance of these aspects ('why'), and collaborate on developing a strategy for future actions ('moving forward'). These questions are invaluable as they concentrate solely on how you can enhance your performance in your current role.

- **How has my performance been over the last few months?** This question sets the stage for a review of your recent contributions and achievements.
- **What are some things that I have done well?** Recognizing your strengths not only boosts morale but also clarifies what behaviors and actions should be continued or amplified.
- **Where can I improve?** Identifying areas for improvement is crucial for personal development and demonstrates your willingness to evolve.
- **Why is that important to our business?** Understanding the broader impact of your roles and

responsibilities links your performance to the company's success.

- **What do I need to do moving forward?** This question is about action—defining clear steps to capitalize on strengths and address areas for improvement.

By concentrating on these questions, you're not only showing a proactive stance on self-improvement but also aligning your personal growth with the organization's goals, which is essential for professional development and potential future discussions about compensation

Economic Value
These questions are strategically designed to help you understand the quantitative measures of success within your organization, allowing you to align your contributions with the company's key performance indicators. Here's a refined explanation for each question:

- **What metrics do you look at when determining how we are performing in our business?** This question aims to uncover the broader performance indicators that your boss considers critical for assessing the company's health and success.
- **What metrics do you use to measure someone's value in our business?** By asking this, you seek to understand the specific criteria used to evaluate individual contributions, providing clarity on how your performance is assessed.
- **What metrics are most important to you in the business?** This inquiry helps prioritize your efforts by identifying which metrics are deemed most crucial

by your boss, allowing you to focus on areas that significantly impact the business.

- **Are there any metrics I could help improve?** This proactive question demonstrates your eagerness to contribute to the company's success, asking for opportunities where your efforts can directly influence key metrics.

Recording these questions and their answers will offer you concrete benchmarks to gauge your economic value within the company. Understanding where to access these metrics and how you can impact them is crucial. By identifying a specific metric you can influence, you illustrate your direct contribution to the company's economic value. Additionally, discerning which metrics are most important to your boss helps you align your efforts with their priorities, enhancing your visibility and value in the organization.

Cultural Value

These questions are tailored to understand the intangible aspects of your workplace, focusing on cultural values and characteristics that define an ideal employee within your organization. Here's an enhanced explanation for each question:

- **How do you measure culture in our business?** This question seeks to uncover the metrics or indicators your boss uses to assess the company's cultural health, providing insights into the intangible aspects that influence the organization's environment.
- **What values do you wish more people expressed at work?** By asking this, you aim to identify the specific values your boss believes are essential for fostering a positive and productive workplace, offering a

blueprint for the behaviors and attitudes valued in the organization.

- **If you could define the perfect employee using three characteristics, what would they be?** This inquiry helps pinpoint the traits your boss considers most critical for success in your workplace, offering a targeted set of attributes to aspire to and demonstrate.
- **How can I help improve the culture of our business?** This proactive question shows your commitment to contributing positively to the workplace environment, seeking actionable ways you can influence the company's culture.

Understanding the cultural expectations and valued characteristics helps you align your behavior and contributions with your boss's vision, positioning you as a key player in shaping the organizational culture. If you embody the traits of the 'perfect employee,' you're not only enhancing your value within the team but also laying a solid foundation for future discussions about compensation.

Regarding the straightforward question about increasing your income:

How can I make more money in our organization?

After establishing a comprehensive understanding of performance and cultural expectations, it's reasonable to inquire directly about advancement and compensation opportunities. This question cuts to the chase, seeking a clear, actionable plan for financial growth within the company. If your boss provides a specific strategy, you can focus your efforts on meeting those targets to enhance your earnings potential.

3. **Get Results**: Because of the first two steps, you now understand the actions you need to take to set yourself up for success. Use the answers you obtained from your boss to achieve the results you need. Create value for your organization to enhance your own value.

   My advice is not to rush. I've often seen people aiming to do just the bare minimum to secure a raise or to tick a box, and it was apparent that there was little effort behind their work. They were doing only what was necessary to achieve their desires, and ultimately, it wasn't sufficient. Avoid setting a time limit on achieving the results you need. Establish a goal and diligently work toward it, regardless of the time required.

   Document your milestones, accomplishments, and breakthroughs as you progress. Keep a journal of your journey to achieve your goals. Firstly, it's beneficial to journal and reflect on your experiences later. Looking back at a success story is also rewarding. Secondly, maintaining a detailed record of your activities is crucial. You will need this information when you request a raise.

   You are ready for the next step once you have accomplished what is necessary to obtain a raise.

4. **Ask for a Raise**: The final step is to schedule a follow-up meeting with your boss to discuss a raise. When they inquire about the purpose of the meeting, it's okay to be upfront and say it concerns a raise.

   The key here is that you've already put in the effort to enhance value for both the organization and yourself. Consequently, requesting a raise should not require elaborate tactics. To prepare for this meeting, revisit your initial discussion with your boss regarding how you can contribute economic and cultural value to the organization and your own growth. Also, go through the notes documenting your achievements and performance improvements. It's essential to showcase your results and demonstrate the value you've added to the organization.

You are ready for the meeting once you have clear notes showing your value. In the meeting, you can structure the conversation very simply:

> **Introduction** - At the beginning of the conversation, ask for a raise. You can also add how much of a raise you would like in this part of the conversation. But you need to get to the point and ask for a raise. Then, say you would like a raise because you have added value to the business.

> **The Proof** - In the middle part of the conversation, dive into the evidence of how you've added value to the business. You will use the notes you took from the first meeting and your notes of proven results to communicate how you've added value to the business.

> **Conclusion** - Wrap up by summarizing that you've added value to the business, and because of that, you would like a raise. At this point, the conversation can go in any direction, but by following this structure, you've set yourself up for success.

When you ask for a raise, be sure to *ask* for a raise. Remain respectful and professional. You are not commanding a requirement but asking them a question. Raises aren't guaranteed, but adding value to the organization makes you much more likely to get a raise.

PROVING MY VALUE

I wanted to get a raise, so I followed the plan I laid out above. First, I met with my boss to gain clarity on what was valuable to our business. For my role, that included drive-thru metrics, customer scores from surveys, and cleanliness.

I got to work, focusing on creating drive-thru systems that made ours one of the top in the state. In the drive-thru, you must balance hospitality, service speed, and order accuracy. Our scores in all three areas were superb.

Then, I turned my attention to our customer metrics, particularly how attentive and courteous our team was and the cleanliness of the restaurant. I made significant improvements in both areas.

Lastly, I analyzed all these metrics and demonstrated that the numbers improved significantly under my leadership. After my initial meeting to identify areas for value addition, I applied what I learned, gathered proof, and documented everything in a notebook. I was proud of my achievements.

The challenging part was asking for a raise. It felt awkward even to initiate a conversation about it, as discussions about money were typically "hush-hush" and seemed taboo. If you're dealing with similar feelings, it's crucial to push through, although that's easier said than done. The confidence to overcome these obstacles comes from solid proof. If you've followed the steps outlined in this chapter, you possess the necessary evidence to request a raise. My thorough preparation gave me the confidence to overcome my fears and request a meeting.

During our discussion, despite the nervousness, I started by stating my desire for a raise. As I referenced my notebook, my confidence grew, bolstered by the tangible evidence of the value I had added. By the end of our meeting, after presenting my case, I asked for a raise again, this time with more assurance. And I received the raise I had requested. My boss commended my efforts and was pleased to grant the raise, acknowledging my valuable contributions and hard work. What a significant victory!

YOUR NEXT STEPS

- ☐ **Schedule a Meeting with Your Boss:** If you want your first raise, schedule your meeting with your boss today! Don't waste another moment wondering how you can add value to your organization and get a raise.
- ☐ **Add Value to Your Business:** This is a prerequisite for getting a raise.
- ☐ **Ask for the Raise!**

There is another way to add economic and cultural value to your business. When you do this, it's easier to get a raise than by asking for one. In the next chapter, you'll learn how to get your first promotion.

CHAPTER 9

HOW TO GET A PROMOTION

"Things do not happen. They are made to happen."
– President John F. Kennedy

I DESERVE A PROMOTION

My first promotion didn't come when I expected it to. It was later than I had planned. I mentioned this in an earlier chapter, but I had a clear plan when I started my first job at Chick-fil-A: to work in the Front of House, excel, learn the ropes, and earn a promotion within a year. Being highly motivated and driven, I thought it would be straightforward.

However, like most things in life, it didn't go as planned. As I mentioned in Chapter 2, my plan was disrupted. Instead of working in the Front of House, I was reassigned to the Back of House. I worried this would delay my planned promotion, cause confusion, and obscure my strengths.

Although being moved to the Back of House might have postponed my promotion slightly, as I've previously stated, it ultimately turned out to be beneficial for me.

I will fill in a small gap I left in my previous story. When I transitioned from the Back of House to the Front of House, where I initially started, I wasn't immediately promoted. A position became available, and I assumed it was destined for me, which I believed was the reason for my reassignment. However, to my surprise, the promotion was granted to someone else. While I don't want to come across as arrogant, I genuinely felt the promotion was undeserved.

In my view, I was more skilled and more deserving of the promotion than the individual who received it. I had diligently followed my bosses' instructions, adapted to various roles, and maintained a positive attitude throughout. I was a collaborative team member whose performance consistently yielded good results. Thus, it was baffling to be overlooked for the promotion, especially after seeing who was chosen.

Adding to my frustration was the suspicion that the decision was influenced by personal relationships rather than merit. For the first time in my professional life, I witnessed what appeared to be a biased promotion based on friendship rather than performance.

This experience led me to a point of apathy in my job at the restaurant, a sentiment you might already be familiar with. The question arose: why bother trying if my efforts would only result in being overlooked? This apathy soon evolved into a series of persistent questions. I was eager to understand the reasoning behind their decision. Was there something I did or didn't do that justified their choice?

I longed for a clearer understanding of the criteria used for promotions. Knowing exactly what qualities they sought in a team leader could have either helped me present a stronger case for myself or prevented my disappointment. If only I had the strategy I'm about to share with you, it might have better positioned me for a promotion.

HOW TO ASK FOR A PROMOTION

I want to highlight the quote at the beginning of this chapter.

> "Things do not happen. They are made to happen."
> - President John F. Kennedy

Nothing can be truer than this. Things hardly ever just happen. Someone or something has to make it happen. Things are rarely just given to people. They are taken by people. This is the mindset I want to focus on as we talk about getting your promotion. Promotions are rarely just handed out. Promotions are made to happen by people taking action to make them happen.

The first action I took, and the first action you can take to set yourself up for a promotion, is to use all the tools in your tool belt. They will make you stand out as the best employee and team member you can be. You've already read about seven tools that can set any employee up for success in any job. Before I wanted a promotion, I was taking advantage of unexpected opportunities, being flexible and curious. I fought apathy not to burn out and hit the wall at work. I built a personal brand of excellence but remained coachable. I accepted feedback as a gift.

The first step in setting yourself up for a promotion is to use the tools you've learned in this book to be the best employee you can be. These are tangible steps to set yourself up for success and make things happen. Whenever my opportunity finally did come for a promotion, I was ready because I had been using my tools to be a good employee.

The second thing to keep in mind with promotions is that promotions come out of a need that arises in the business. The first need a business has is the need to get a leader. They want to have a minimum number of leaders according to their unique requirements, and finding someone to fill that position becomes necessary if they don't have enough leaders. The second version of a need is better for you: they need *you* to lead. This need comes because you have performed so well that the business feels like they will miss out if you are not in leadership.

Both business needs can benefit you if you take the necessary action to be the best employee you can be. When you are performing at a high level, and a position becomes available, the business will almost always turn to its high performers first to fill that spot. Whenever you perform at an exceptionally high level, many businesses will feel like they are missing out or will lose you if they don't make you a leader. Again, both can work to your benefit. You prepare the same way for both needs.

Let's get into the nitty-gritty. Whenever the business isn't coming to you and asking you to be a leader, what other action can you take to make things happen? Well, you can ask for a promotion. What does this process look like? It's going to look very similar to how you ask for a raise.

1. **Meet with Your Boss:** Schedule the meeting again. If you report to multiple supervisors, choose the one with the greatest influence over the promotion you're aiming for. Inform them that the meeting's purpose is to discuss what it takes to be a leader within the organization. This approach not only allows your boss to prepare adequately but also demonstrates your proactive attitude.

   You might find this initial step familiar, as it mirrors the action we took previously when seeking a raise. However, I cannot emphasize enough the power of simply asking. Actions, and particularly promotions in this context, are often the result of showing initiative. By making your presence felt and your intentions clear, you position yourself favorably for success.

2. **Clarify Leadership Needs:** During your initial meeting with your boss, it's crucial to gain clarity on what they seek in a leader. Understanding their expectations is vital as it could either alter your perspective or diminish your interest in the role. The latter scenario is beneficial, as it prevents you from pursuing a position that could lead to dissatisfaction and apathy.

   It's equally important to ensure you're not focusing your efforts in the wrong direction. Avoid striving to excel in areas that aren't valued in the leadership role you're eyeing. Remember, the competencies required for leadership often differ significantly from those needed for entry-level positions.

   Be diligent in taking notes during this discussion. Inquire about the top three qualities they value in a leader and how they assess these traits. While this may seem repetitive if you've read the previous chapter, the process bears similarity for a reason. Establishing a clear understanding of what's expected in a prospective promotion enables you to demonstrate that you're the ideal candidate based on their specified criteria. Your goal is to make your suitability for the role unmistakably clear.

3. **Get Results:** After your meeting, transform your notes into a detailed action plan. With your boss's criteria for leadership and their methods of evaluation in hand, you're positioned to excel. Develop a strategy outlining the necessary steps to meet the desired leadership qualities. Establish measurable objectives to track your progress toward meeting the key metrics.

Pursue the best outcomes possible without constraining yourself with a strict timeline. Focus on goal-oriented milestones instead. Utilize the insights from your boss to define precise, quantifiable targets within your action plan, and persist until you achieve them. Document your accomplishments meticulously. Your aim is to demonstrate unequivocally that the organization would be at a disadvantage without you in a leadership role.

Bear in mind that success doesn't occur by chance; it's the result of deliberate efforts. By devising a plan and securing tangible results, you're not just waiting for opportunities—you're actively creating them.

4. **Ask for a Promotion:** Regardless of whether a promotion is currently available or not, now is the time to express your interest and request the promotion. If a position is open, seize the opportunity! Adhere to the application procedure specified by your organization. The distinguishing factor in your success throughout the application and interview stages will be your preparedness, equipped with quantifiable achievements demonstrating why you are the superior candidate compared to others.

If the position is not open, now is your chance to create a business need. Now is your opportunity to show your business they are missing out by not having you as a leader. Meet with your boss, express interest in being a leader, and show them how you best fit the role, given *their* criteria.

During this journey, embodying both confidence and humility is crucial, though it may seem paradoxical. It's important to differentiate between confidence and cockiness; the former is a positive trait, while the latter is not. Cockiness stems from an overblown sense of one's abilities or importance, which contradicts humility. On the other hand, confidence aligns with humility and is based on tangible evidence of your capabilities.

Your confidence should be rooted in the knowledge and skills you've acquired, along with the tangible results you've achieved. This assurance should stem from the tools and strategies you've learned, ensuring you've done all you can to position yourself for success. If you find your confidence wavering, focus on enhancing those areas until your self-assurance is solidified.

When discussing potential promotions, your confidence—or lack thereof—will be apparent. If you're genuinely confident in your skills and accomplishments, let that confidence show in your conversations. However, this confidence should be tempered with humility, a quality you've already learned is vital in maintaining coachability in the workplace.

Approaching the promotion process with humility prevents confidence from veering into arrogance. Be proud of your achievements, but remain grounded and respectful throughout.

If your efforts culminate in a promotion, that's a wonderful outcome, and it's a testament to your hard work and dedication. However, if the promotion doesn't materialize, don't be disheartened. As illustrated by my own experience, not every attempt at advancement will succeed on the first try. Persist in your efforts, continue to refine your skills, and remain proactive. The more you establish yourself as a valuable asset, the more indispensable you become to the business.

FINALLY PROMOTED

Reflecting on the situation, I realize the immense value of the plan I've since developed. Had I implemented it earlier, I wouldn't have been left guessing about the leadership qualities sought by my superiors, and I could have positioned myself as the prime candidate for advancement. Despite feeling overlooked initially, that episode wasn't the conclusion of my journey.

I continued to leverage every tool at my disposal, striving to be the exemplary employee I knew I could be, independent of others' actions. I championed my personal brand and became an invaluable contributor to the organization.

Later, I took the step I should have taken earlier: I met with my boss for clarity on what they valued in a leader and inquired about the rationale behind the other individual's promotion. Armed with this new understanding, I dedicated myself to aligning with these expectations and began to track my progress against the set standards, aiming to embody the leadership traits they desired.

Opportunity struck a few months later. In an unexpected turn, two team leaders, including the one promoted over me, abruptly resigned one evening, leaving immediate vacancies. Upon arriving for my shift that following Monday, I was ushered into training to fill one of these leadership roles.

This sudden chance arose, and I was prepared. Although I didn't orchestrate the circumstances, I had made myself the optimal candidate for when the moment arose. Earning my first promotion was a moment of immense pride, not just for the title, but for the effort and growth it represented. While this advancement brought its own set of challenges and responsibilities—topics for another discussion—I was thrilled to step into a leadership role at my first job, proud of the groundwork I had laid to turn possibility into reality.

YOUR NEXT STEPS

- ☐ **Show Up Well:** Do your current role well. You'll never get promoted if you aren't good at your current job, so make sure you are being the best employee you can be.
- ☐ **Ask and Clarify:** Meet with your boss and get clarity on what it takes to move up in your organization.
- ☐ **Get promoted!**

Congratulations on your perseverance and commitment to personal and professional growth. By mastering the tools that demand significant time to learn and implement, you've demonstrated remarkable resilience and adaptability. Your ability to seize unforeseen opportunities, maintain flexibility and curiosity, and overcome apathy speaks volumes about your dedication.

You've also successfully crafted a personal brand and embraced a mindset of continual learning, recognizing the value of remaining coachable at every stage of your career. By viewing feedback as an invaluable resource, you're well-equipped to navigate the challenges of requesting your first raise and vying for your first promotion.

Now, we're about to explore the final tool, the most crucial concept I'll introduce in this book. This tool is the capstone of all the strategies you've learned, designed to solidify your foundation for sustained success and fulfillment in your career.

CHAPTER 10

HAVE FUN

"If you're not having fun, you're not doing it right."
- S. Truett Cathy

FORGETTING TO HAVE FUN

I consider myself to be a fun individual, yet I recognize that work has its own distinct sphere. My drive and competitive nature are intense. When I started experiencing success at work, it became an exhilarating addiction. My focus shifted entirely toward enhancing my performance and eagerly anticipating the next opportunity, always looking ahead to my future steps.

Two years into my tenure at Chick-fil-A, while I was pursuing a business degree, I began reflecting on how much I enjoyed my job. Was it possible to carve out a long-term career at Chick-fil-A, a job I hadn't initially sought but had embraced due to an unexpected opportunity? This question led me to explore various career paths within the company.

The role of an Owner/Operator, the franchisee of a restaurant, seemed particularly enticing. The idea of being my own boss and running my own Chick-fil-A was alluring. I believed I had the necessary knowledge—or at least I thought I did—to manage a restaurant successfully.

Alternatively, the corporate path beckoned. Residing in metro Atlanta, I had the opportunity to visit the Support Center several times, where I discovered fascinating roles. These teams were tasked with creating solutions that could potentially benefit all 3,000 restaurants, not just one.

Eventually, I decided to pursue a career at the Support Center, driven by two main reasons: my love for college football, which made me reluctant to work Saturdays in the long term, and my belief that my skill set was more aligned with large-scale operations. This marked the beginning of my journey toward a corporate career, starting from my humble beginnings in the company.

Transitioning from my initial job to a full-fledged career demanded time, dedication, continuous learning, and relentless effort. I became entirely engrossed in planning my career progression, which became my foremost priority at work. After seven years of dedication, I attained my goal—a position at the Support Center, a testament to my hard work and perseverance.

Yet, upon reflection, I recognize a vital element I overlooked: the sheer fun of working at Chick-fil-A, which initially ignited my desire for a career there. Despite various obstacles and moments of doubt, the underlying joy remained a constant, fueling my drive for improvement and success. I wish I had acknowledged that my journey was not only about advancement but also about cherishing the enjoyable moments along the way.

In the following sections, I will share strategies to help you stay present and find joy in your work, ensuring you don't overlook the fun that can accompany professional growth.

ENJOY THE RIDE

I commenced this chapter with a quote from Truett Cathy, the founder of Chick-fil-A, because his words and the company he built have significantly influenced my life. The moment I decided to delve into the topic of having fun at work, I knew a quote from Truett Cathy would be a perfect fit.

The quote I selected is displayed in numerous Chick-fil-A restaurants, often alongside an image of Truett hula-hooping. Truett was not only an astute businessman who understood the intricacies of profit-making and advocated for fiscal prudence and diligence in company growth, but he also appreciated the value of joy and amusement in the workplace.

My fondness for the TV show "The Office" is another source of inspiration for me. I've watched the entire series multiple times, and despite finding seasons 8 and 9 less appealing, the series finale always moves me, especially as an "Office" enthusiast. One poignant moment is when Andy Bernard, portrayed by Ed Helms, delivers a line that resonates deeply:

> "I wish there was a way to know you're in the good
> old days before you've actually left them."

In this reflective moment, Andy contemplates his experiences at the office, recognizing the invaluable times spent with colleagues and friends. As he acknowledges the end of his chapter at Dunder Mifflin, he expresses a nostalgic longing for the days that have passed.

If you find joy in your work, continue to embrace and share that happiness with those around you. Everyone merits the opportunity to experience a workplace that's not only productive but also enjoyable. If you're fortunate enough to recognize the 'good old days' of your career while you're living them, cherish and make the most of those moments.

If you are like me, and struggle to have fun at work and enjoy the moment, here are some steps you can take to have more fun at work:

1. **Enjoy the View:** Viewing your job and career as a mountain climb is a compelling metaphor. It places your first job at the base of the mountain, marking the start of an upward journey. It's crucial, however, to occasionally halt your ascent, look around, and appreciate the scenery—enjoying the view is an integral part of the journey.

    If you perceive your job as part of this upward climb, taking a moment to observe your surroundings serves as a vital break, encouraging you to pause and find enjoyment in the moment. It's easy to become overly focused on the summit, constantly fixated on the distance yet to cover, as I once was. Instead, make a conscious effort to stop and appreciate how far you've come.

    As you ascend the mountain of your career, each step upward offers a new perspective, while the view behind you changes and eventually disappears. Therefore, it's important to savor the view at every stage of your climb. Equally important is to cherish the company of the people who are on this journey with you. Their presence can enhance the experience, turning what could be a solitary trek into a shared adventure full of memorable moments and shared achievements.

2. **Look How Far You've Come**: For the hyper-achievers among us, the inclination to continuously gaze upward, fixating on the

summit of our career mountain, is a common trait. It's a drive that keeps us motivated, always assessing the distance to our ultimate career goals. While this forward-looking mindset is beneficial for motivation, it can also detract from living in the present and experiencing joy in our current achievements.

If you've tried to heed the advice from the first step—to relish the view and the moment—but find it challenging because your focus is invariably drawn to 'what's next,' consider a piece of wisdom a friend shared with me late in my journey:

"If I could go back in time and show myself three years ago where I am right now, I would be blown away."

This perspective was a game-changer for me. It suggested that instead of always looking up, I should occasionally shift my gaze downward, acknowledging the ascent I've already accomplished. This approach helps in appreciating the present, making it easier to savor the moment and find enjoyment in your current position.

By recognizing how much you've ascended, you not only celebrate your progress but also allow yourself to enjoy your current standing more fully. This acknowledgment can be a powerful tool in balancing the drive for future achievements with the capacity to find joy and satisfaction in the now, thus enriching your overall journey up the career mountain.

3. **Journal**: Although initially not keen on journaling, I embraced it early in my tenure with Chick-fil-A, recognizing the start of my professional journey. My initial intent was to document successes and failures, providing a resource for learning and reflection. While this approach has its merits, I encourage you to take a slightly different path with journaling.

Focus on capturing the enjoyable moments at work. For instance, if a closing shift turns out to be particularly amusing, or a colleague's joke brings a smile to your face, jot down these experiences. If a harmless error leads to laughter, include that too. Journaling these instances allows you to relish the moments as they occur and to revisit the joy they brought later on.

This practice isn't just about keeping a record; it's a tool to ensure you're consciously acknowledging and valuing the fun aspects of your job. It prompts you to recognize and appreciate the enjoyable experiences, likely leading you to discover that there are numerous moments worth noting each week. Embracing this form of journaling can highlight that your first job—or any job, for that matter—can and should be a source of enjoyment and not just a stepping stone in your career path.

If the previous suggestions didn't quite resonate with you because you naturally find joy in your work without the constant drive to focus on the next milestone, that's perfectly fine! Your ability to effortlessly find fun in your workplace is a wonderful trait, and I encourage you to spread that positivity around. First jobs hold the potential to be among the most enjoyable experiences in your career, offering opportunities to form bonds that could last a lifetime.

It's entirely possible to balance personal growth, contribute to business improvements, and have a great time simultaneously. Excelling in your first job doesn't have to be a solemn endeavor; it can be the most enjoyable time you spend working. So, embrace the fun at work. Cherish and revel in those joyful moments as they happen. Remember, it's important not to overlook the value of the present—the good old days you'll look back on fondly are happening right now. So, make the most of them, share your joy with others, and help create an enjoyable and uplifting environment for everyone.

THE GOOD OLD DAYS

During my tenure at my first job, my eyes were always set on the future, keen on climbing the career ladder quickly and excelling in my role. The destination was my primary focus. Now, having reached my goals at Chick-fil-A, I find myself reflecting much like Andy Bernard from "The Office" did.

While I was indeed having fun at work, I didn't fully embrace those joyful moments as they unfolded. It's only upon looking back years later that I fully appreciate the extent of enjoyment my job brought me. This realization has prompted me to want to share stories of the fun I experienced, highlighting that work isn't just about achievements and progress—it's also about enjoyment and creating memorable moments.

Waffle House
Growing up in Atlanta, I was no stranger to Waffle House, an iconic 24/7 breakfast spot. My first experience of it as a gathering place came when a colleague, during my night shifts, suggested we unwind there after work. We often spent hours enjoying each other's company, laughing, and sharing stories. Even though these gatherings extended late into the night, making mornings come all too soon, the joy and camaraderie we shared became fond memories I cherish.

Football
I love football. I played it growing up, and my passion for the game has led me to host a football podcast. As I developed friendships with my coworkers, we began playing football after closing on some nights. There was a green space behind our restaurant, illuminated by streetlights, that was perfect for our games.

This activity fostered teamwork and efficiency among us, as the game could only start once everyone had finished their closing duties.

Consequently, many of us would pitch in to help our coworkers complete their tasks, allowing us all to get to the game quicker.

Inside Jokes

I've lost count of the times I've been reduced to tears of laughter at work. On one occasion, while using headsets to take drive-thru orders, we found ourselves in a particularly silly mood late at night. We spontaneously decided to sing our communication to a customer instead of speaking. Perhaps it wasn't the most conventional approach, but amusingly, the customer sang his order back to us. Delighted by his spirited response, we rewarded him with free food for brightening our night.

On another memorable evening, a colleague creatively fashioned a large, brown paper bag into a makeshift Sorting Hat from Harry Potter. He humorously used it to assign our roles for the evening. The image of him donning the Sorting Hat in the kitchen still brings a smile to my face every time I see it.

Christmas Party

For two straight years, one of my best friends and I got to host the Christmas party for our restaurants. Of course, working for Chick-fil-A, the party happened on a Sunday. We decided to do a "Tonight Show" style dinner show and create sketches based on Jimmy Fallon's popular nighttime broadcast. We replicated sketches from the show such as "Thank You Notes," and "Box of Lies," and even had our own monologue.

We prepared for over a month, both times, to ensure that the entertainment for our party was funny and enjoyable for the team. Hosting those Christmas parties is one of my most fond memories of working at Chick-fil-A, and getting to do it with one of my best friends made it even better.

Travel
I had the opportunity to travel across the country on my company's dime, exploring cities I'd never visited, experiencing sporting events in stadiums I'd longed to see, and introducing Chick-fil-A to new communities. During my travels, I met someone who would become a lifelong friend and who, fatefully, introduced me to my future wife.

She was working for Chick-fil-A in another city, and our paths crossed thanks to a mutual friend connected through our jobs. Thus, I owe not just a wealth of experiences to my first job but also my marriage, which has been an incredible journey of its own.

Lifelong Friends
About three years after getting married, I realized that all five groomsmen in my wedding had worked with me at Chick-fil-A simultaneously. I met my best man through our job, connecting over our shared passion for Georgia Football. Our time at Chick-fil-A also brought me closer to people I had known before, thanks to our shared experiences at work.

Recently, I caught up with the guys from Chick-fil-A, and we found ourselves reminiscing about "the good old days" and how much fun that period of our lives was. Despite the long workdays, challenging people and situations, and late nights, we had each other's company to share those experiences. I enjoyed both the good and the challenging times because I was with lifelong friends.

I had a tremendous amount of fun at my first job. Looking back, I wish I had savored those moments more instead of just reflecting on the fun I had later. It's important to do both. So, enjoy your first job. Have fun!

YOUR NEXT STEPS

- ☐ **HAVE FUN!** Make memories, goof off, laugh, and have a good time at your first job.
- ☐ **Enjoy the View:** Look around and enjoy each moment you create. You only get a first job once.
- ☐ **Journal:** Write down your experiences to savor them in the moment and the future.

Congratulations! You have now learned ten ways to master your first job. While working on your mastery, don't forget to have fun along the way.

CONCLUSION

YOUR FIRST JOB MASTER'S DEGREE

Congratulations on finishing this book! You now possess the tools to excel in your first job and advance your career. If you've reached this point, I consider you to have a "Master's Degree" in your first job opportunity. Very few people put in the effort to maximize their first job, and by reading this book, you've demonstrated your commitment to developing into a better leader.

- **Seize unexpected opportunities at work.** Take calculated risks by preparing for the unexpected, evaluating your options, and seeking wisdom from others.
- **Be flexible.** Enhance your adaptability by managing what you can control, influencing what you can, and releasing what is beyond your control or influence.
- **Cultivate curiosity at work.** Being inquisitive can open doors—ask insightful questions, take initiative, and don't shy away from trying new things.

- **Combat apathy.** It can be detrimental both in life and at work, so actively fight against it. Seek assistance when needed, engage in exciting projects, and rely on supportive work relationships.
- **Develop your personal brand.** Identify, refine, and represent your brand effectively. Disregard distractions and maintain a high standard of excellence.
- **Remain coachable.** Even the world's top athletes continue to learn and improve—embrace humility, listen openly, and foster a growth mindset.
- **Treat feedback as a gift.** Whether giving or receiving feedback, clarify what it entails, understand its importance, and devise a plan for action.
- **Aim for your first raise and promotion!** Opportunities are made, not stumbled upon. Arrange meetings with your supervisor, demonstrate tangible results, and confidently request that raise or promotion.

Above all, enjoy your first job—you only get one. It should be a source of fun and a chance to create lasting memories and friendships. My first job was an incredible part of my journey, and I hope yours will be too.

The next steps are yours to take. Knowledge is useless without action. Remember, success is created, not waited for. I encourage you to use what you've learned and actively make things happen.

Apply the strategies from this book to excel at work and use your first job as a stepping stone for your career. Now, go out there and master your first job!

ACKNOWLEDGMENTS

I want to thank the following people who all helped me on my career journey. Each of you had an impact on me. You all helped me master my first job, turn it into a career, and launch my own business. Thank you for the impact you had on my life.

Garrison B.	Autumn K.
Michael C.	Evan K.
Morgan C.	Karyna K.
Chris D.	Gage M.
Rachel D.	Jennifer M.
Andrew E.	Josh M.
Wes G.	Cole O.
Daniel H.	Caleb P.
Evan H.	Blake R.
Justin H.	Brittany R.
Rachel H.	Graham R.
Ron H.	Austin S.
Shea F.	Jeremy S.
Hunter I.	Caleb T.
Joshua J.	Nathaniel T.
Andrew K.	Kirby W.

ABOUT THE AUTHOR

Meet Jacob Karnes, the dynamic founder of Waves Business Coaching and the engaging host of the Waves Business Coaching Podcast. As a Business Made Simple Certified Coach, Jacob is passionate about providing clear, straightforward strategies to empower individuals in their careers, starting with their very first job.

Jacob's journey to success began at Chick-fil-A, where he not only excelled in the restaurant but also made significant contributions in the corporate office over a span of ten years. At Chick-fil-A, Jacob honed his skills, learned the value of hard work, and discovered the principles that would later become the foundation of his coaching philosophy.

Drawing on his wealth of experience and a deep desire to make a meaningful impact, Jacob has crafted a book that distills his insights into practical, actionable tools designed to help you thrive from the get-go. Whether you're stepping into your first job or looking to refine your approach to work, Jacob's guidance is an invaluable resource for building a successful career.

Now, from his home base in Atlanta, Georgia, Jacob continues to inspire and guide through his business and podcast, alongside his wife, Addi, and their daughter, Jamie. Embark on your journey to career mastery with Jacob Karnes and discover how to transform your first job into a launchpad for lifelong success.

WORK WITH JACOB

Bring the best out of your team.

Keynotes
"Jacob's session was incredibly healing and insightful for me." - Emma M.

Workshops
"Jacob has a wonderful way of causing you to lean in as he unpacks the principles in his workshop." - Grant Y.

Coaching
"I've been blown away with how quickly having an outside perspective has transformed my business operations and direction. Jacob is the real deal, and I wish I had hired them a year sooner." - Michael C.

Work with Jacob:
MasterYourFirstJob.com/Work

LEAVE A REVIEW

Thank you for reading my book!

I would love your feedback so that I can make my future books better. After all, Feedback is a Gift. :)

5.0

Please take two minutes to leave a review on my book.

You can leave a review here:
MasterYourFirstJob.com/Review

Thank you!

Printed in Great Britain
by Amazon

61995044R00077